Exploiting Small Advantages

EDUARD GUFELD

B.T.Batsford Ltd, *London*

First published 1985
© Eduard Gufeld 1985

ISBN 0 7134 4822 9(limp)

Photoset by Andek Printing, London
and printed in Great Britain by
Billing & Sons Ltd,
London, Guildford & Worcester
for the publishers
B.T.Batsford Ltd, 4 Fitzhardinge Street,
London W1H OAH

A BATSFORD CHESS BOOK
Adviser: R.D.Keene, GM
Technical Editor: P.A.Lamford

Contents

Introduction

The idea of writing a book on this topic occurred to me back in my youth. I recall how in a certain tournament two 'venerable' candidate masters agreed a draw in the following position *(1)*:

At first sight there was nothing surprising in this, since the position appears completely drawn. And yet White has an original way to win: 1 c6+! ♔e7 2 ♔c5 ♔d8 3 ♔b4! ♔c8 4 ♔b5 ♔b8 5 ♔c5! ♔a7 6 ♔d4 ♔a6 7 ♔e5 ♔b6 8 ♔d5 ♔a6 9 ♔e6, and the king invades decisively at d7.

It was only much later that I learned that a similar winning method had been found by the remarkable Soviet analyst Nikolai Grigoriev.

There is undoubtedly a close and mutually fruitful connection between study composition and endgame theory. But a study is an artificial work. The composer's ideas are embodied only after lengthy analysis and searchings, which are crowned by a happy discovery. But to find a single, study-like way to win under practical playing conditions is extremely difficult.

A modern-day chess game very often demands precise mastery in exploiting a minimal advantage. In a battle between two players who are roughly equal in strength, the accurate and by no means straightforward realization of a small advantage is practically the only chance of gaining a win. It is a long time since the era of dashing attacks, the result of which was often the creation of unsightly pawn islands. The standard of average players has grown considerably, enabling them to compete fairly competently and surely against opponents who are slightly superior to them in practical strength, experience and knowledge. And therefore a mastery of typical methods of exploiting a minimal advantage is a necessary condition for achieving success.

It is well known that two types of advantage exist in chess – material and positional (later we will touch on another, highly interesting but little-studied type of advantage – psychological). The chess classicists asserted, not without reason, that to win it is necessary to have a combination of both forms of advantage. But what about those cases where only one is present? Then the way to victory becomes a narrow path, often hard to find, between a practical game and a study.

The reader may object that, even with a small and equal number of pieces on the board, positions can be found in which a positional advantage alone ensures a win. This cannot be denied, and it is sufficient to imagine a typical finish to a pawn ending with a passed pawn on each side *(2)*:

However, in such situations the enormous difference in the placing of the pieces makes the positional advantage of one of the sides practically overwhelming.

Good endgame technique has long been valued in chess, and has been an attribute of all outstanding players from the past and the present.

Players even with only slight experience know what comprises endgame technique. The works of major endgame theorists are a great help in mastering the secrets of the endgame, and success in this is required by any player as he seeks to improve.

1   Exploiting a Small Positional Advantage

How often we meet situations where one of the sides possesses a small positional advantage! In game commentaries we read time and again: " . . . the insignificant advantage (usually positional) is hardly sufficient for a win", or "by energetic moves Black neutralizes White's slight positional advantage".

It may also happen differently – by a series of energetic moves an insignificant positional advantage may be converted into a win, but only because the defending side failed to exploit sufficiently his defensive resources. In short, the concept of positional advantage is a very broad one.

Of course, it is not our idea to cover all aspects of this problem. Rather than rules, we will be more interested in exceptions, in positions verging on a draw, where at times everything is decided by one move.

For greater clarity, the examples are arranged according to material, which may have a certain methodological value.

QUEEN ENDINGS

Timman-Larsen
Montreal 1979

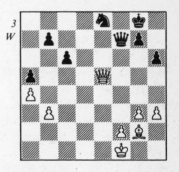

White's positional advantage results from the more active placing of his pieces and the insecurity of the black king's shelter. The pawns at b7 and c6 are under fire from the white-squared bishop, and are therefore qualitatively devalued. Black is faced with a difficult defence.

1	♗e4	♔f8
2	♕xa5	♕xb3
3	♕c5+	♔f7
4	♗c2	♕d5
5	♕b4	

Timman skilfully probes the new weaknesses in the opponent's position, while retaining prospects of an attack on the black king.

5	...	♕d7
6	♗b3+	♔g6

6 ... ♔f6 loses immediately to 7 ♕f8+ with inevitable mate.

7	♕e4+	♔f6
8	♕h4+	♔g6
9	♕e4+	♔f6
10	♔g2	♘c7?!

Black should have decided on 10 ... g5!.

11	♕f4+	♔e7
12	♕b4+	♔d8
13	♕xb7	

White's positional advantage has been transformed into a material one.

13	...	♕d3
14	♕b4	c5!
15	♕c4!	

This transition into a minor piece ending is the quickest way to win.

15	...	♕xc4
16	♗xc4	♘e8
17	♔f3	♔c7
18	a5	♘d6
19	♗d5	♔b8
20	♔f4	♔a7
21	♔e5	♘b5

22	♗c4	♔a6
23	♔d5!	

23 ♗xb5+ ♔xb5 24 ♔d5 c4 25 a6 c3 26 a7 c2 27 a8♕ c1♕ 28 ♕b7+ would also have won, but the move played is more precise.

23	...	♔xa5
24	♔xc5	♘c3
25	♗d5	♘d1
26	f4	♘f2
27	♔d4!	

The active king is decisive!

27	...	♔b4
28	♗f3	♘xh3
29	♔e3	g5
30	f5	g4

30 ... ♔c5 also fails to save the game after 31 ♗g4 ♘g1 32 ♗f2 h5 33 ♗xh5 ♘h3+ 34 ♔f3!.

31	♗xg4	♘g5
32	♔d4	♔b3
33	♗h5	♔c2
34	f6	♔d2
35	f7	♘e6+
36	♔e5	♘f8
37	♔d6	

1-0

This is how Timman's win appears 'schematically':

1. Creation of new weaknesses in the opponent's position in parallel with threats to the black king.

2. Transformation of a positional advantage into a material one.

3. Transition into a won minor piece ending.

Very simple, wouldn't you agree?!

Ljubojević-Karpov
Linares 1981

The Yugoslav grandmaster Ljubojević is a player with an aggressive, attacking style. The play in a 'dull' ending such as this is hardly to his taste. The pawn formation suggests to us that the game opened with the fire-proof Caro-Kann Defence, and after mass exchanges an ending has arisen in which Black has a slight positional advantage – his knight is qualitatively superior to the opponent's bishop. By subtle manoeuvring, Black methodically increases his minimal advantage and converts it into a win. At this point it is important for him to decide on a clear-cut strategic plan and to seize the initiative, by gradually building up threats. Karpov carries out this difficult task in vituoso style.

1	...	g6!
2	hg	fg
3	a3	a5!

In the first instance the opponent must be deprived of possible counterplay.

4	b3	h5
5	♕e4	♘f5
6	♗f2	♕d7

Now Black has control of the d-file, but for the moment there are no invasion squares.

| 7 | a4 | ♔c7! |
| 8 | ♔c2 | |

The pseudo-active 8 ♕a8 would have allowed Black to increase his advantage still more: 8 ... ♕d3! 9 ♕a7+ ♔c8 10 ♕a8+ ♔d7 11 ♕b7+ ♔e8 12 ♕b8+ ♔f7 13 ♕b7+ ♘e7.

| 8 | ... | ♕d8! |

The queen has to be activated, and to this end the undermining ... g5 is highly appropriate.

9	♔c1	g5!
10	fg	♕xg5+
11	♔c2	♘e7!

11 ... ♘xg3? 12 ♗xg3 ♕xg3 13 ♕h7+ and 14 ♕xh5 would have led to an equal position.

| 12 | ♕h7 | ♔d7 |

The immediate exchange of queens by 12 ... ♕g6+ also came into consideration. Here too Black evidently retains a significant advantage, but he wishes to exchange the queens under the most favourable circumstances.

13	♕e4	♕f5
14	♕d3+	♔c6
15	♕xf5	ef
16	♗e3	♘g6

17   e6

This pawn is doomed. White's last chance is to break through with his bishop to the opponent's queenside pawns.

17	...	♔d6
18	♗g5	♔xe6
19	♔d3	f4!
20	gf	h4
21	♔e3	h3
22	♔f3	♔f5
23	♔g3	♘xf4!
24	♗d8	

The pawn ending – 24 ♗xf4 h2 – is hopeless for White.

24	...	♘e2+
25	♔xh3	♘d4
26	♗xb6	

No better is 26 ♔g2 ♔e4 27 ♔f1 ♔d3 28 ♔e1 ♘xb3 29 ♔d1 ♔xc4 30 ♔c2 ♘d4+ 31 ♔b2 ♘e6.

26	...	♘xb3
27	♗d8	♔e4
28	♔g4	♔d4
29	♔f4	♔xc4
30	♔e4	♔c3!
31	♗f6+	♔c2
32	♗e5	c4
33	♔e3	c3
34	♗f6	♘c5
35	♔e2	

After 35 ♔d4 ♘xa4 36 ♔c4 Black would have had to play accurately: 36 ... ♘b6+ 37 ♔b5 a4 and wins, but not 36 ... ♘b2+? 37 ♔b5 a4 38 ♔b4, saving the draw.

35	...	♔b3

0-1

**Gheorghiu-Larsen
London 1980**

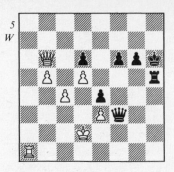

White must first concern himself over the safety of his king, and only after this will he be able to exploit his passed b-pawn, or, after the c4-c5 break, his d-pawn. Gheorghiu finds a very elegant solution to this problem.

1	♔c3	♖h3
2	♔b4	

Under cover as quickly as possible, especially since the e3 pawn is poisoned: 2 ... ♕xe3 3 ♕xe3 ♖xe3 4 b6, and the passed pawn decides matters.

2	...	♕f2
3	♖a3!	

The rook defends its king excellently from the rear.

3	...	♕b2+
4	♔a4	♕c2+
5	♔a5	♕d2+
6	♔a6	♕b4
7	♖a5	

Now Black tries to steal up on the enemy king from the other side, but equally unsuccessfully.

	7	...		♚g5
	8	c5!		♖h8

The exchange of queens leads to a hopeless position: 8 ... ♕xc5 9 ♕xc5 dc 10 b6, while after 8 ... dc the d-pawn cannot be stopped.

	9	♕c6		♖d8
	10	b6		dc
	11	b7		c4
	12	♖b5		♕a3+
	13	♚b6!		f5

13 ... ♕xe3+ is met by 14 ♚c7!.

	14	♕c5		

1-0

It will hardly be any great revelation if I state that the king is the most active piece in the endgame. In the next few examples the king proves to be exceptionally mobile in queen endings, where it takes offensive action against ... the queen herself.

Gufeld-Spiridonov
Tbilisi 1970

White has a slight positional advantage, in the form of the more active position of his centralized king, and, very important, his superior pawn formation (fewer pawn islands!).

	1	♚e4		♕c2+

Black's defence is also very difficult after 1 ... ♕g2+ 2 ♚e5! ♕c6 3 ♕g5. The attempt to set up a defence by 1 ... ♕a5 does not produce any tangible result after 2 ♕g5. Incidentally, another advantage for White is the fact that, after the exchange of the black c5 pawn for the white b3 pawn, White's pawn on the c-file can reach the queening square much more quickly than the black a-pawn. Yet another example supporting the opinion that queen endings are very similar to pawn endings.

	2	♚d5		♕f5+
	3	♚d6		♕f6+
	4	♕e6		♕d4+

The pawn ending after 4 ... ♕xe6+ 5 ♚xe6 ♚h6 6 ♚d5 ♚h5 7 ♚xc5 ♚h4 8 ♚d6 is hopeless for Black.

	5	♚c6		♕c3
	6	♕e7+		♚h6
	7	♕f8+		♚h7

After 7 ... ♚h5 White captures on c5 with check.

	8	♕xc5		♕f3+
	9	♕d5!		♕xb3
	10	c5		

Black's position is lost. 10 ...

♕xh3 is not possible due to 11 ♕d7+, while 10 ... ♕a4+ is met by 11 ♔c7, when the c-pawn has a clear road forward.

Here a paradoxical incident occurred, whose source is most probably to be found in the distant chess past, when they announced "check" when attacking the king, and "guardez" when the queen was threatened. Here my opponent 'mixed up' which of his main pieces White was attacking ...

10	...	♔h6??
11	♕xb3	
	1-0	

Gufeld-Raskin
USSR 1976

The winning path abounds in interesting subtleties. We all know from our own experience how cunning are these queen endings. The No. 1 problem facing White is to deploy his queen in its most active position.

| 1 | ♕f2 | ♕d7 |
| 2 | ♕f3 | |

With a glance at the h5 square.

| 2 | ... | ♔g6 |
| 3 | ♕a8 | |

Aiming for g8. If 3 ... ♕d3+ 4 ♔h4.

3	...	♔g7
4	a4	ba
5	ba	♕d3+
6	♕f3	♕d2

Black has defended as well as possible, but . . .

| 7 | ♕g2! | |

The white queen sets up an ambush.

7	...	♕e1+
8	♔h2+	♔f7
9	♕b7+	♔g6
10	♕c6	

This 'quiet' move decides matters. The black queen cannot give check – there follows 11 ♕g2+, exchanging queens.

| 10 | ... | ♔f7 |

Now the e-pawn falls.

11	♕d7+	♔f8
12	♕d8+	♔f7
13	♕f6+	♔g8
14	♕xe6+	♔g7
15	♕f6+	♔g8
16	♕g5+	♔h8
17	♕d8+	♔g7
18	♕d4!	♔f7
19	♔g2	

The white king has no objection to taking a walk to g5.

| 19 | ... | ♔f8 |

20	♕d3	♔e7
21	♕xf5	

1-0

An instructive ending, wouldn't you agree?

Bangiev-Kuzin
USSR 1968

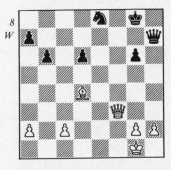

Usually in the endgame a queen and knight are stronger than a queen and bishop – thanks to their greater manoeuvrability. But in this example White has a slight advantage, due to the centralized placing of his pieces and his kingside pawn majority. His plan now includes advancing his g- and h-pawns, so as to restrict still further the mobility of the opponent's pieces.

1	g4!	♕e7
2	♔g2	♕e6!

Sensible tactics – Black tries to set up a defence on the white squares.

3	a4	d5!
4	h4	♘d6

5	♔h3	♘e4
6	♕f4	

With the queens on the board it is difficult for White to count on realizing his minimal advantage. His main trump is his passed pawn on the kingside, which can be used most effectively in the minor piece ending.

6	...	♕d6

The exchange of queens is forced, since with his last move White had created some pretty dangerous threats – 7 ♕h6 and 7 ♕b8+.

7	♕xd6	♘xd6
8	♔g3	♘c4

Black cannot play his king to e6, since this allows White to organize a pawn breakthrough: 8 ... ♔f7 9 ♔f4 ♔e6 10 ♔g5 ♔f7 11 ♔h6 followed by 12 ♔h7, then g4-g5 and h4-h5.

9	♔f4	a6
10	♔g5	♔h7

The white king must not be allowed to reach h6.

11	♔f6	b5
12	ab	ab
13	♔e6	b4
14	♔xd5	♘a3
15	c4	bc
16	♗xc3	♘b5
17	♗e5	

The knight is in danger – it must be urgently evacuated to the kingside. Will this succeed?

| 17 | ... | ♘a3 (9) |

9
W

18 ♔e6!

The knight cannot be caught, but it is driven to the edge of the board, and the white king acquires maximum activity.

18 ... ♘c4
19 ♗f4

Black has a pretty draw after 19 ♗d4? ♘d2 20 ♔f7 ♘f3 21 ♗f6 g5! 22 hg ♘e5! 23 ♗xe5 – stalemate!

19 ... ♘b2
20 ♔f7 ♘d3
21 ♗d6?

With victory in sight, White makes a mistake. The natural 21 ♗g3 would have allowed him to put into effect his basic winning mechanism – the breakthrough of his g-pawn. It was essential to deprive the knight of the f2 square. After 21 ♗g3! ♔h6 22 ♔f6! ♔h7 23 g5 or 22 ... g5 23 ♗d6! (excluding once again the possibility of stalemate – 23 hg+ ♔h7 24 ♔f7 ♘e5!) White wins.

21 ... g5?

Black too fails to rise to the occasion. 21 ... ♔h6! was essential,

when after both 22 ♗g3 g5! 23 ♔f6 gh 24 ♗xh4 ♔h7, and 22 ♔f6 ♘f2! 23 ♗f8+ ♔h7 24 g5 ♘e4+ 25 ♔f7 ♘g3! he gains the desired pawn.

22 ♗g3?

A further mistake. White could have won by 22 ♗h2 or 22 ♗b8.

22 ... gh
23 ♗d6

White can even lose the game here: 23 g5? hg 24 g6+ ♔h6 25 g7 ♘e5+ 26 ♔f8 ♘g6+ 27 ♔f7 ♘e7!.

23 ... h3??

The loser is the one who makes the last mistake. There was still a draw by 23 ... ♔h6! 24 ♔f6 ♘f2 25 g5+ ♔h5 26 g6 ♘g4+ 27 ♔f7 ♘h6+. The mistakes towards the finish by both sides can be explained only by fatigue from the difficult struggle in this ending.

24 g5

At last! The g-pawn will become a queen. **Black resigned.**

Gufeld-Damjanović
Skopje 1972

10
W

"White is a piece up!" you will say. Yes, but to realize it is far from simple. White cannot get by without a pawn breakthrough. But the straightforward plan with f2-f3 and g3-g4 leads to an impasse after the exchange on g4: if he plays h4-h5, he creates the wrong passed pawn – h8 is a black square and his bishop is the white-squared one.

Imagine that the queens are removed from the board. Then the win becomes easy. White's king embarks without hindrance on a victorious journey towards e7, e8, f6, and Black inevitably ends up in zugzwang.

Disregarding this factor, the first part of White's plan is to activate his queen and bishop to the maximum extent, while for the moment his king assumes the role of an interested observer.

1	♗c6	♕d6
2	♕b7	♕f8
3	♕b2	

With the idea of becoming entrenched at f6.

3	...	♕c5
4	♗e4	♕e7
5	♕e5	

The threat is 6 ♕xh5+. It is obvious that 5 ... f5 is bad for Black – this would leave his e-pawn doomed.

5	...	♔g8
6	♕g5!	♕e8

6 ... ♕b4 is bad due to 7 ♗xg6.

7	♕f6!	♔h7

Black is in an unusual form of zugzwang, and is forced to mark time with his king within a small space. It is now that White embarks on a pawn storm against His Majesty's fortress.

8	g4	hg
9	h5	♔h6
10	hg	fg

The enemy bastions have been blown up and reduced to ruins, and now the white king emerges from his residence with decisive intent.

11	♔g3	♔h7
12	♔xg4	♔h6
13	f4	

The pawn boldly steps forward, to sacrifice itself.

13	...	♔h7
14	♔g5	♕b5+
15	f5	ef
16	♕f7+	♔h8
17	♔h6	

Unconditional surrender. **Black resigned**.

MULTI-PIECE ENDINGS

Suetin-Gufeld
Tbilisi 1970

The game was adjourned in this position, and Black sealed 1 ... ♗xb4. Analysis showed that Black should be able to maintain the

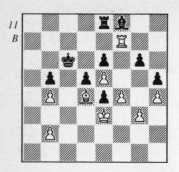

11
B

balance, although achieving the draw is not without its difficulties.

2	♖f6	♔d7
3	♖xg6	♖c8
4	♖g7+	

4 f5 ef 5 ♔f4 ♗c5! is not dangerous for Black.

4 ... ♔e8

Only not 4 ... ♗e7 5 b4!, when White has an enormous advantage.

5 ♖g8+

On 5 f5 there follows 5 ... ♖c2.

5	...	♔d7
6	♖g7+	♔e8
7	♖g8+	♔d7
8	♖xc8	♔xc8
9	g4!	

This exclamation mark is not attributed to the move itself, which should not have upset the equilibrium on the board. I attribute it to the splendid fighting qualities of Alexei Suetin, who even in a drawn position seeks latent paths to continue the struggle.

9 ... hg

10 ♔f2! *(12)*

In the event of 10 h5 ♗f8 11 ♔f2 ♗h6 12 ♔g3 ♔d7 13 ♔xg4 ♔e7 the draw is obvious.

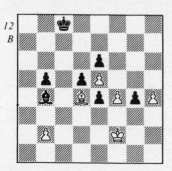

12
B

I of course analysed this position at home, but did so carelessly – with the black king at d8 . . .

Here I began moving instantly, thinking that Suetin had made a mistake leading to defeat.

10 ... ♗d2

10 ... ♔d7 was the simplest.

11 ♔g3 e3

Black gains an easy draw by 11 ... ♔d7 12 h5 ♔e7, when 13 h6 ♔f7 14 h7 ♔g7 15 f5 ♔xh7 is unfavourable for White, while after 13 ♔xg4 ♔f7 14 f5 ♗c1 he cannot strengthen his position.

12	h5	e2
13	♗f2	e1♕
14	♗xe1	♗xe1+
15	♔xg4	♗b4
16	h6	♗f8
17	h7	♗g7 *(13)*

The last few moves have been forced. Here the game was again adjourned, with Black sealing his last move 17 ... ♗g7. A genuinely study-like situation has arisen.

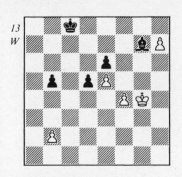

18   ♔g5   d4

18 ... ♗h8 19 ♔g6 merely transposes. 18 ... ♔d7 is much worse, since after 19 ♔g6 ♗h8 20 ♔f7 d4 21 f5 d3 22 fe+ ♔c7 23 e7 d2 24 e8♕ d1♕ 25 ♕xh8 Black does not have perpetual check.

19   ♔g6!   ♗h8
20   f5   d3
21   fe   d2
22   e7   d1♕

This is already Black's third queen in this one game!

23   e8♕+   ♕d8

After 23 ... ♔c7 24 ♕xh8 Black does not have perpetual check: 24 ... ♕g4+ 25 ♔f7 ♕h5+ 26 ♔e7 ♕h4+ 27 ♔f6 ♕xh7+ 28 ♔f8.

24   ♕c6+   ♔b8

Black loses after 24 ... ♕c7 25 ♕xc7+ ♔xc7 26 e6.

25   ♔f7!! *(14)*

A brilliant move!

25   ...   ♔a7

The only move, since 26 ♕d6+ was threatened, and on 25 ... ♗xe5 White wins by 26 ♕xb5+ and 27 ♕xe5.

26   ♕d6   ♕c8

Black fails to draw after 26 ... ♕g5 27 ♕c7+ ♔a8 28 ♕c8+ ♔a7 29 ♕xh8.

27   e6   ♕c2
28   e7!   ♕xh7+
29   ♔e8   ♗xb2
30   ♔d8   ♕h4
31   ♔c8?!   ♕e4!

The black pieces also show their 'teeth'. 32 ♕d7+ ♔b6 33 e8♕? is not possible due to 33 ... ♕a8 mate.

32   ♕c7+?   ♔a6
33   ♕d6+   ♔a7?

It is probably that after 33 ... ♔a5! Black would have had every chance of a draw. For his part, two moves earlier White should have played 31 ♕d7+, reaching the position which occurs in the game.

34	♔d8	♕h4
35	♕d7+	♔b6
36	♕e6+	♔b7?

Here too 36 ... ♔a5! was still possible, with hopes of saving the game.

37	♕d5+!	♔b6
38	♔d7	♕h7
39	♕e6+	♔a7
40	♔c8!	

If 40 ♕a2+, then 40 ... ♔b6 41 ♕xb2? ♕f5+ with a draw.

40	...	♕c2+
41	♔d8	♔b7!?
42	♕d7+	♔b8
43	♕d6+	♔b7
44	e8♕	♗f6+
45	♔d7	

and within a few moves **Black resigned**.

Gufeld-Furman
Moscow 1970

15
W

In view of the fact that his b3 and c4 pawns are doomed, White must act very energetically. His immediate task is to break through

with his rook onto the 7th rank.

1	♖a5	♖c8
2	♖xa6	♗xb3
3	♖a7	g6
4	♖g7+	♔f8
5	♖xh7	♖c6

The next step in the plan is to create a passed pawn on the kingside.

6	♖b7	♗xc4
7	h4	♖c8
8	g4	♗d5

Black establishes contact between his rook and bishop.

9	♖h7	♖a8
10	h5	gh
11	g5!	d3

A diversionary pawn advance, but, alas, it does not save the game.

12	g6	d2
13	♔e2	♗xf3+
14	♔xd2	♗e4
15	♔e3	♗d5
16	♖xh5	♔e8
17	♖h8+	♔e7
18	♖h7+	

1-0

After 18 ... ♔e8 19 ♗f6 e5 20 ♖e7+ ♔f8 21 ♖xe5 and 22 ♖xc5 further resistance becomes pointless.

Kasparian-Simagin
Sochi 1952

The position on the board is a technical draw, and in Simagin's place many players would not

have bothered wasting time and energy, but would have immediately signed a peace agreement.

By his play in this game Simagin gives a useful lesson to many young players, who at an early stage strive to conserve their creative energy.

"Battle on, as long as there is the slightest chance", is what he seems to be saying, "and sooner or later you will be suitably rewarded."

1	...	a5!

Frightening White with the threat of opening the a-file.

2	g6	h6
3	♘f4	♘xf4
4	♗xf4	♖fe8
5	♖f2	a4
6	♖c1	b4
7	♖e1	♗e6
8	h5	♖a8
9	♖ee2	

Overprotecting in advance the weakness at c2.

9	...	♔g8!

Such moves, which outwardly are in no way noteworthy, often have a strange effect on the opponent, prompting him without good reason to play actively. With his last move Black shows that he is not in a hurry, and intends to improve the position of his king. And although the transfer of the king to the centre does not create any specific threat, Kasparian decides to complicate matters.

10	♔g3	♔f8
11	♗c1	♖a6!

Sensing the opponent's 'mood', Simagin does not forestall his plan. Otherwise Black could simply have exchanged on b3 and prevented the advance prepared by White.

12	a3?	

This pseudo-active move makes it more difficult for White to gain a draw.

12	...	ab
13	ab	♖a1!

White obviously overlooked this intermediate blow.

14	♗b2	♖g1+
15	♖g2	♖h1!
16	♖h2	♖d1
17	bc	bc
18	♖xc2	♖xd3+
19	♔f4	

The white king's position is already giving certain cause for alarm. Note that the alternative

19 ♔f2 would have been no better:
19 ... ♗d5!.

19	...	♖b8
20	♖cd2	♖e3!

The culminating point of the struggle. In this objectively still drawn position Simagin sets his opponent a difficult problem. He threatens ... ♖bb3 with mate, and 21 ♗xd4 ♖e4+ or 21 ♖xd4 ♖bb3 22 ♖f2 ♖h3! is obviously unsatisfactory.

All that remains is to move one of the rooks to e2. But which one? This is the difficulty facing White.

| 21 | ♖de2? | |

The apparently forces the black rook to exchange or retreat, but it is here that Simagin's brilliant idea is revealed. The way for White to save the game was by 21 ♖he2!.

| 21 | ... | ♖b4! |
| 22 | ♖xe3 | (17) |

22 ... d3+!!

Black sacrifices a whole rook, but the offer cannot be accepted:

23 ♔f3 ♗d5+ 24 ♔f2 ♖xb2+ 25 ♔g3 f4+!.

23	♖e4	♖xe4+
24	♔g3	f4+
25	♔f3	♗d5!

Black's positional advantage has become a reality, and the presence of opposite-coloured bishops merely makes White's defence more difficult.

26	♔g4	f3+
27	♔g3	♖c4
28	c6	

So as somehow to complicate matters.

28	...	♔e7!
29	♖d2	♗xc6
30	♖xd3	♖c2
31	♗a3+	♔e6
32	♖d1	

Bad is 32 ♖d6+ ♔f5 33 ♖xc6 ♖xc6 34 ♔xf3 ♖c3+.

32	...	f2
33	♗f8	♗b5
34	♗xg7	f1♕
35	♖xf1	♗xf1
36	♗xh6	♗e2
37	g7	♔f7
38	♔h4	♖c6!
39	♗f4	♔xg7
40	♔g5	♗d3
41	♗e3	♔f7
42	h6	♔e6
43	♗f4	♗h7

0-1

Simagin created a genuine study in a practical game against an eminent study composer!

Reti-Rubinstein
Göteborg 1920

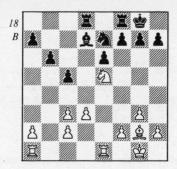

The knight at e5 looks highly imposing, but in the given position the weakness of White's queenside pawns is of much more significance. By the following subtle manoeuvre Rubinstein emphasizes this.

1	...	♗a4!
2	♖e2	♘d5
3	♗xd5	

This exchange makes White's defence more difficult. He should have decided on 3 c4!?, when after the possible 3 ... ♘b4 4 ♖c1 f6 5 ♘f3 White has a passive but sound position. Now, however, the superiority of Black's bishop over the enemy knight becomes very marked.

3	...	ed
4	♖ae1	♖fe8
5	f4	f6

The exchange of rooks favours Black. Rubinstein has made a deep assessment of the minor piece ending which now ensues.

6	♘f3	♔f7
7	♔f2	♖xe2+
8	♖xe2	♖e8
9	♖xe8	♔xe8
10	♘e1	

The knight is forced to take up a passive post, and now the black king gains the chance to break into the opponent's position along the weakened white squares.

10	...	♔e7
11	♔e3	♔e6
12	g4	

Otherwise Black plays 12 ... ♔f5 and then by the advance of his h-pawn weakens White's kingside pawns.

12	...	♔d6
13	h3	g6
14	♔d2	♗d7!

The bishop copes splendidly with its mission. The threat to the c2 pawn is now ineffective, so it sets its sights on the pawns on the opposite wing.

15	♘f3	♔e7!!

Excellently played. The hasty 15 ... h5 would have allowed White to ease his defence by 16 g5 fg 17 ♘xg5. It is by such moves that one senses the hand of a true maestro!

16	♔e3	h5!
17	♘h2	

Forced: after 17 gh gh 18 h4 ♔e6 Black's king breaks through to the white pawns.

17	...	♔d6

18   ♔e2   d4!

Depriving the white king of the important e3 square, and fixing White's pawns on squares of the same colour as the bishop. Black has the future possibility of playing ... g5 and invading with his king via e5.

19   cd   cd
20   ♔d2   hg
21   hg

The pawn ending is hopeless for White: 21 ♘xg4 ♗xg4 22 hg g5!.

21   ...   ♗c6!
22   ♔e2

The attempt to free his game by 22 c3? leads White to a sad and highly instructive end: 22 ... dc+ 23 ♔xc3 ♗g2! 24 ♔d4 b5 25 ♔e3 a5 26 a3 ♔d5 – zugzwang.

22   ...   ♗d5!
23   a3   b5
24   ♘f1   a5

By forcing White to play a2-a3, Rubinstein has acquired the possibility of creating a passed pawn on the a-file.

25   ♘d2   a4
26   ♘e4

White tries unsuccessfully to save himself in the pawn ending, but 26 ♔d1 g5! would equally have left him no chance.

26   ...   ♗xe4
27   ed   b4
28   ♔d2   ba
29   ♔c1   g5!
                0-1

Rubinstein's play in this ending gives truly aesthetic pleasure.

Spassky-Ljubojević
Montreal 1979

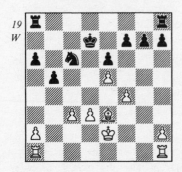

Black's position looks quite safe – he has no pawn weaknesses, and he has fair prospects on the half-open d- and c-files. It would seem that Ljubojević too assessed this ending fairly optimistically – at first he does not make any attempt to create counterplay. But in fact White has a significant positional plus – a compact and potentially mobile pawn mass in the centre. The first part of White's plan is to remove the obstructing pawn at b5, which has to be made into a weakness.

1   ♖hb1!   ♖ab8
2   ♗c5   ♖hc8
3   ♗d6

This bishop has no obvious target to attack, but its unpleasant 'X-ray' effect is already felt – the mobility of the black pieces is restricted.

3	...	♖b7
4	a4	♘d8
5	ab	ab
6	♔d2	f6

Rather belated activity. White has already given his opponent a weakness at b5 and he controls an important strategic line – the a-file.

7	d4	♘f7
8	♗b4	fe
9	fe	♘h6
10	♖a5	♘f5
11	♔d3	g6

Black has set up something of a fortress on the white squares, which Spassky now sets about destroying.

12	♗c5	♖cb8
13	♖a6	♖c8
14	♔e4	♖cc7
15	♔f4	

By the threat of the king's invasion at f6 White forces a weakening of the opponent's kingside pawns.

15	...	h6
16	♔e4	g5

Black is in zugzwang. On 16 ... ♖c8 there follows 17 d5 ed+ 18 ♔xd5 ♘e7+ 19 ♗xe7 ♔xe7 20 ♖e6+ ♔f7 21 ♖f1+ ♔g7 22 ♖ff6, winning.

17	♖ba1	♖c8
18	♖xe6!	

A highly elegant solution – Black's seemingly impregnable fortress collapses.

18	...	♖xc5

Of course, 18 ... ♔xe6 19 ♖a6+ and 20 ♔xf5 is also hopeless.

19	♔xf5	♖xc3
20	♖xh6	

The game is decided, White's connected passed pawns in the centre being irresistible.

20	...	♔c7
21	♖h7+	♔b6
22	♖xb7+	♔xb7
23	e6	♔c7
24	♖a7+	♔b6
25	♖a8	

1-0

The following game by the great Capablanca is an excellent text-book example on the theme of the 'positional squeeze'.

Capablanca-Yates
New York 1924

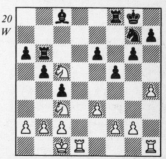

20
W

White's position is better – he controls the d-file and the black pieces are passive, but the presence of a large number of pawns makes Black's position fairly 'viscous' and stable. Capablanca's next brilliant move has the aim of weakening the opponent's queenside pawn chain, after which the scope of the white knights is increased.

1	a4!!	♞h5
2	b3	cb
3	cb	ba
4	♞3xa4	♜c6
5	♔b2	♞f6

Trying to suppress White's activity after a possible doubling of rooks on the central file.

6	♜d2	a5

One can understand Black's desire to remove this pawn from its vulnerable position, but at a5 too it will not be easy to defend. 6 ... ♔f7 was more flexible, trying to impart greater stability to the position and improve the co-ordination of the pieces. Remember one of the basic rules of chess – do not advance pawns on the wing where the opponent is stronger.

7	♜hd1	♞d5
8	g3	

Capablanca's entire subsequent play is a brilliant example of a methodical and purposeful positional squeeze.

8	...	♜f7
9	♞d3!	♜b7
10	♞e5	♜cc7
11	♜d4	

After the inevitable e3-e4 the backward e6 pawn will become another appreciable weakness in Black's position.

11	...	♔g7
12	e4	fe
13	♜xe4	♜b5
14	♜c4!	

Capablanca does not avoid exchanges, rightly assuming that his positional advantage is stable.

14	...	♜xc4
15	♞xc4	♝d7
16	♞c3!	♜c5
17	♞e4	♜b5
18	♞ed6	♜c5
19	♞b7	

The pursuit of the rook by the knight is highly entertaining.

19	...	♜c7
20	♞bxa5	♝b5

The black pieces have revived somewhat, but this is only a temporary phenomenon.

21	♞d6	♝d7
22	♞ac4	♜a7
23	♞e4	

The knights in this game 'work' splendidly.

23	...	h6
24	f4	♝e8
25	♞e5	♜a8
26	♜c1	♝f7
27	♜c6	♝g8
28	♞c5	♜e8
29	♜a6	♜e7
30	♔a3	♝f7
31	b4	

Capablanca has strengthened his position to the maximum, and now it is the turn of the b-pawn.

31	...	♞c7
32	♜c6	♞b5+
33	♔b2	♞d4
34	♜a6	♝e8
35	g4	♔f6
36	♞e4+	♔g7
37	♞d6	♝b5
38	♜a5	♝f1
39	♜a8!	

White prepares a mating net: 40 ♞e8+ followed by ♞f6+ and g4-g5. Black's reply is forced.

39	...	g5
40	fg	hg
41	hg	♝g2
42	♜e8	♜c7

Black also loses after 42 ... ♜xe8 43 ♞xe8+ ♔f8 44 g6 ♔xe8 45 g7.

43	♜d8	♞c6
44	♞e8+	♔f8
45	♞xc7+	♞xd8
46	♔c3	♝b7
47	♔d4	♝c8

Black is ready to give up his minor pieces for the white pawns and obtain a theoretically drawn position, but Capablanca is inexorable.

48	g6	♞b7
49	♞e8!	♞d8
50	b5	♔g8
51	g5	♔f8
52	g7+	♔g8
53	g6! *(21)*	

1-0

The final position undoubtedly deserves a diagram:

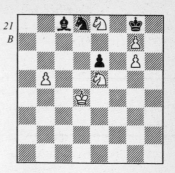

Black is in complete zugzwang – neither his knight nor his bishop can move due to inevitable mate.

To conclude this section devoted to multi-piece endings, we will analyze the finish to a game between two modern grandmasters. It is to be hoped that their battle will give pleasure to the reader, since one of the co-authors, Lubomir Kavalek, remarked that ". . . playing over this game is more entertaining than reading a detective story".

Larsen-Kavalek
Montreal 1979

A prosaic and rather tedious endgame position, wouldn't you agree? Black's chances are no worse – he has a passed pawn, the bishops are of opposite colour, and in general there is little material on the board. But what comprises the skill of a genuine master is the fact that he can 'breathe life' even into such positions, and will persistently seek the slightest tactical nuances for continuing the struggle. To those pessimists who assert that the endgame is a rather tedious pursuit, we advise that they should again and again play through this ending, in which a fascinating and uncompromising struggle develops.

1	g4!	fg
2	hg	h6
3	♖g6	♘c5

Only three moves have been made, and what was not apparent at first has become obvious – White has a fairly appreciable positional advantage.

4 ♘g3!

With his small army Larsen succeeds in creating dangerous threats against the enemy king.

4	...	♗d4+
5	♔f3	b4
6	♘f5+	♔f8
7	♖b6!	

Accuracy is essential. The h6 pawn is doomed, but the b-pawn

has to be controlled.

7	...	♗c3
8	♖b8+	♔f7
9	♘xh6+	♔e7
10	♘f5+	

The position has clarified. White's chances are associated with exploiting the insecure position of the black king and with the advance of his connected passed pawns (the g-pawn is especially dangerous). Black's one, but sufficient counter-chance is his passed b-pawn, supported by active pieces.

10	...	♔d7
11	♘e3	♖d4
12	♗f5+	♔c6
13	g5	♘d3
14	♘g2	♖d5!
15	♗e4	♔c7!

Black defends very resourcefully.

| 16 | ♖g8 | ♖d4 |
| 17 | ♖g6 | |

The further advance of the g-pawn suggests itself, but in fact this eases Black's defence – 17 g6 ♘c5 18 g7 ♖xe4 19 ♖c8+ ♔xc8 20 g8♕+ ♔c7.

17	...	♔d7
18	♖b6	♘c5
19	♗f5+	♔c7
20	♖b5	♔c6
21	♖b8	♘d7
22	♖e8	♘c5
23	g6	♖d2

Playing such an ending is no less difficult than working out a forcing combination. The cost of a single mistake is too high.

24	♘e3	♘d3
25	♘g4	

25 ♖e6+ came into consideration.

25	...	♖d1
26	♖c8+	♔b7
27	♔e2	♖d2+
28	♔e3	♘e1!

Black activates his pieces to the maximum.

29	♖c4

The f-pawn requires defending.

29	...	♘g2+
30	♔e4	♘h4
31	♗c8+	♔b8
32	f5	♖e2+
33	♔d5!	

The only move to retain the advantage. 33 ♔d3 is well met by 33 ... ♖e8!.

33	...	♖d2+
34	♔e6	♖d4 *(23)*

23
W

Note the placing of the pieces. All White's are on white squares, and all Black's on black squares.

White should now have disturbed this set-up and played 35 ♖xd4 ♗xd4 36 ♘f6, but he misses this possibility, and Black obtains excellent drawing chances.

35	♗a6	♘xf5!!
36	♔xf5	♖d5+
37	♔e4	♖g5
38	♗c8	♖xg6
39	♘e3	♖h6
40	♔d5	♗d2
41	♘f5	♖b6

A draw has become very much a reality, and all that is required of Black is accuracy.

42	♘d6	b3
43	♗f5	

The game enters its concluding phase. White has still not exhausted all his attacking resources against the enemy king, and the opposite-coloured bishops assist his plan.

43	...	♗b4
44	♘f7	b2
45	♗b1	♗a3
46	♖c3	♖b7!
47	♘e5	♖b5+
48	♔e6	♗b4
49	♖b3	♔c7?

Here it is, the fatal mistake. Black could still have held the draw by 49 ... ♖b6+.

50	♘d7	♔d8
51	♗e4	♖a5
52	♘e5	

52 ♖xb4 ♖a6+ 53 ♖b6 was much simpler.

52	...	♖a6+
53	♘c6+	♔c7
54	♖xb4	♖b6
55	♖xb6	♔xb6
56	♔d5	♔b5
57	♗c2	

1-0

The dramatic and far from faultless struggle in this ending is another striking confirmation of the fact that there are no tedious positions but only tedious, routine play, which is capable of stifling any position.

ROOK ENDINGS

Any chess player who has tried to improve will probably have spent a considerable time on the study of rook endings. Without a knowledge of this undoubtedly complicated field of chess, it is impossible to imagine any creative improvement. Here too considerable space will be devoted to rook endings. And we will begin by examining two game fragments, the leitmotif of which is . . . mating threats.

In the other games in this section you will see the sacrifice of a pawn for the initiative or for an active king, as well as a number of other typical techniques. We should once again emphasize that in all these examples one of the sides has only a very slight advantage, and it is only his enormous will-to-win and, of course, great skill that enables him to gain the upper hand.

Novak-Ryc
Czechoslovakia 1978

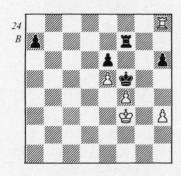

As we glance at this 'simple' position, let's dream a little for White. If the black rook could be driven off the f-file, it would be possible to construct a piquant mate by ♖f6! A good idea, but hardly practicable. But can't we think up a different, more unusual mating construction? We look more closely and see that it is possible. Remove the black pawn from h6, and we can give mate by the rook at g5! Two attractive mating ideas – that must mean something!

Let's see what we can do!

1	...	♔g6!
2	♖e8!	♔f5
3	h4!	a5

Black's rook cannot move – the e6 pawn would be lost, and his h-pawn is also tied to its post – the g5 square! That only leaves the a-pawn.

4 h5!

This pawn will help its rook to reach g6, and then also g5 . . .

4	...	a4
5	♖h8	a3
6	♖xh6	a2
7	♖g6	

1-0

Even the extra queen does not help. The eternal tragedy of one missing tempo . . .

Marić-Petrović
Yugoslavia 1973

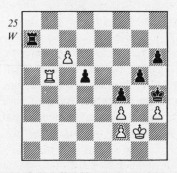

25
W

How can the white pawn be queened – isn't that what you thought, on glancing at this position? But the impression is that this is hardly practicable, and in this you are not deceived. It cannot be queened, but by diverting the opponent's rook into passive defence, we can put Black in an unusual zugzwang position.

| 1 | ♖xd5 | ♖c7 |
| 2 | ♖c5 | ♔h5 |

Black cannot advance his pawns – the white king will break free with decisive effect.

| 3 | ♖c2! | ♔h4 |
| 4 | ♖c1 | |

A step back, so as then to take two steps forward.

| 4 | ... | ♔h5 |

Sceptics may ask: but what if Black nevertheless tries advancing his pawns, is this so bad for him? Let us check: 4 ... h5 5 ♖c4! g4 6 hg hg 7 ♖c5! g3 8 fg fg 9 ♔g1!, and it is all over.

5 h4!!

If the mountain will not come to Muhammad . . . The possibility of a mate from above has already been seen, and now we can see the possibility of one from below – 5 ... ♔xh4 6 ♖h1 mate.

Black can't do anything about it, White has forced him to advance his pawns.

| 5 | ... | g4 |

Black's position is equally hopeless after 5 ... gh 6 ♔h3.

6	fg+	♔xg4
7	f3+	♔xh4
8	♖c5	♖g7+

The only move. 8 ... h5 is met by 9 ♔f2!.

9 ♔f1!

The king begins its famous

'triangular dance', giving the opponent the move.

9	...	♖c7
10	♔f2	h5
11	♔g2	

Once again 'requesting' a check . . .

| 11 | ... | ♖g7+ |
| 12 | ♔f1 | ♖g2?! |

Piquant, but nothing more . . .

| 13 | ♖xh5+ | |
| | **1-0** | |

Jakobsen-Jansson
Stockholm 1974/75

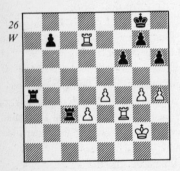

26
W

A very complicated double rook ending. The activity of the white rook at d7 can be countered by the co-ordinated action of both black rooks. Now 1 ♖xb7 is pointless because of 1 ... ♖d4, when the game must end in a draw. Therefore White decides to sacrifice a pawn, to activate his forces to the full. A pawn sacrifice for the initiative occurs no less frequently in the endgame than at

the start of the game!

1	g5!	hg
2	hg	fg
3	♔g3!	

White's two connected passed pawns more than compensate for his slight material deficit, and in addition his king comes actively into play. White's forces have become more mobile, and this proves decisive, although the winning path is by no means straightforward. It should be mentioned that 3 ♖ff7 is weaker due to 3 ... ♖xd3!.

| 3 | ... | b5 |
| 4 | ♔g4 | ♖a8 |

The b-pawn cannot run far: 4 ... b4 5 e5! b3+ 6 ♔xg5 ♖a8 7 e6! ♖c1 8 e7, and White wins.

5	♖f5	♖b8
6	♖xg5	b4
7	e5	♖c1
8	♖gxg7+	♔h8
9	♖h7+	♔g8
10	♖dg7+	♔f8
11	♔f3!!	

A paradoxical decision – realizing that it will be difficult to weave a mating net, White does not hurry with his king to the aid of his rooks, but takes it towards the opponent's passed pawn, having in view the useful exchange of one pair of rooks after ♖b7.

| 11 | ... | ♖c6 |

In the event of 11 ... b3 12 ♖b7 ♖xb7 13 ♖xb7 ♖b1 14 ♔e2! b2 15

&d2 the rook ending is hopeless for Black.

12	♖b7	♖xb7
13	♖xb7	♖c3
14	♔e4	♖b3
15	d4	♖b1
16	♔d5	b3
17	♔e6	b2
18	d5	♔g8
19	d6	

1-0

Rubinstein-Alekhine
Carlsbad 1911

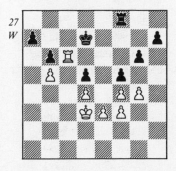

27
W

The rook at c6 is splendidly placed, about that there can be no argument. White's compact and flexible pawn mass in the centre is restricted by the pawns at d5 and f5. If it should now be forcibly advanced, the situation in the centre will clear, and it will be easier for Black to defend.

What then should White do, how can he further strengthen his position? Rubinstein finds an excellent and far from obvious plan of activating his king. One cannot get by in endings without activating the king – this is a law that we have firmly assimilated.

| 1 | ♔e2!! | |

With unhurried haste, the king heads for h4 . . .

1	...	♖f7
2	♔f2	♖f8
3	♔g3	♖e8
4	♖c3	♖e7

The activity of the white rook, which has been forced to defend the e-pawn, has been somewhat reduced, but now the f5 pawn will also require defending.

| 5 | ♔h4 | h6 |

The white king must not be allowed to reach g5.

| 6 | ♔g3! | |

The crafty white king intends to return again to d3. What then was the point of this heroic march? The point is that the advance of the h-pawn has weakened Black's pawn chain on the kingside, and on returning to c6 the white rook will gain total mastery of the 6th rank. By weakening the opponent's position, we at the same time strengthen our own . . .

Realizing that already the game is strategically hopeless, Alekhine provokes a rapid crisis, hoping in this way to gain counterplay.

6	...	h5
7	♔h4!	

The green light for the white

king's path into the opponent's position is again shining . . .

7	...	罩h7
8	♔g5	fg
9	fg	

Not 9 ♔xg6 g3! 10 ♔xh7 g2 11 罩c1 h4, when it is Black who wins.

9	...	hg
10	♔xg4	罩h1!

Activity is Black's last chance of saving the game.

11	♔g5	罩b1

Black can of course defend his g-pawn, but then the white king will go to e5, when it will all be over.

12	罩a3	罩xb5
13	罩xa7+	♔d6
14	♔xg6	罩b3
15	f5	罩xe3

Black has done the maximum possible, but his position remains difficult.

16	f6	罩g3+
17	♔h7	罩f3
18	f7	罩f4
19	♔g7	罩g4+
20	♔f8	罩g1
21	♔e8	罩e1+
22	♔d8	罩f1
23	罩d7+	♔c6
24	♔e8	罩f4
25	罩e7	♔b5
26	罩c7!	

Accuracy is necessary: 26 f8♕? 罩xf8+ 27 ♔xf8 ♔c4, and Black saves the draw. But after 26 罩c7! **Black resigned**. The white king

goes to e5, picks up the d-pawn, and only then returns to the passed f-pawn. Wouldn't you agree that in this game the king worked with inspiration, like a true artist?

**Sokolov-Martinović
Yugoslavia 1973**

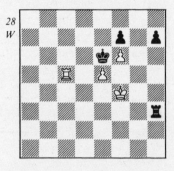

Black's rook is fairly active, and he has a passed pawn, but even so he does not stand well. It only needs White to eliminate the f7 pawn and Black's game will be beyond saving. Easily said, but not easily done.

1	罩c6+	♔d7
2	罩a6	罩h1

2 ... 罩h4+ 3 ♔g5 罩h1 is futile, even though Black seems to have diverted the king. By continuing 4 罩a7+ ♔e8 5 罩a8+ ♔d7 6 罩f8 ♔e6 7 罩e8+ ♔d5 8 e6! White wins.

3	罩a7+	♔e8
4	罩a8+	♔d7
5	罩f8	♔e6

6	♖e8+	♔d5
7	♖d8+!	

'Courteously' inviting the black king to return to e6, where ruination awaits it – 7 ... ♔e6 8 ♖d6 mate.

7	...	♔c6
8	♖d6+	

The persistent white rook has made a considerable achievement – now the black king is driven away from the f7 pawn.

8	...	♔c7
9	♖d3!	

Watch out, the famous 'bridge' may go into operation. The threat is e5-e6!

9	...	♖h5
10	♖a3!	

What's this? White allows the black king to return to the defence of its pawn. What then was the point of all these complicated rook movements? White's aim was to force the black rook to take up a poor position at h5, and now the second cycle of driving the black king away from the f7 pawn decides the game.

10	...	♔d7

Black cannot prevent the white rook from breaking through onto the 7th rank: 10 ... ♔b7 11 ♖g3! followed by ♖g7.

11	♖a7+	♔e8
12	♖a8+	♔d7
13	♖f8	♔e6
14	♖e8+	♔d5

15	♖d8+	♔c6

The 'series' continues with the black rook badly placed at h5.

16	♖f8	♖h4+

Were the black rook at h1, it would be able to bother the white king with checks from below, whereas now it is all much simpler.

We should mention in passing that Black could have won the e-pawn, but this would not have saved the game after 16 ... ♔d5 17 ♖xf7 ♖xe5 18 ♖d7+ ♔c6 19 ♖d3.

17	♔g5	♖h1
18	♖xf7	

At last!

18	...	♔d5
19	♖e7	h5
20	f7	

1-0

The energetic and pretty 'dance' of the white rook creates a strong impression.

Moskalev-Gufeld
Kostroma 1980

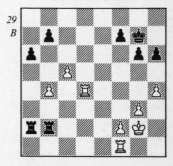

Is Black's slight positional advantage sufficient for a win? It is not easy to answer this question. At any rate, defending in such positions is far from simple. Black can improve the placing of his pieces, whereas White is doomed to passive waiting.

1	...	g5
2	hg	hg
3	♔f3	♖a3+
4	♔g2	♖c3

Black can win the b-pawn, but he does not wish to permit the activating of his opponent's rooks after 4 ... ♖a4 5 ♖e1 ♖axb4 6 ♖d7 followed by the doubling of the rooks on the 7th rank.

5	♔h3	♖cb3
6	c6!?	bc
7	♖c4	♖xb4
8	♖xc6	a5

Black's positional advantage has been transformed into a material one. A new, more complex stage of realization commences.

9	f4	gf

9 ... ♖b6 also came into consideration.

10	♖xf4	♖xf4
11	gf	♖b5!
12	♔g4	f5+!
13	♔g5	

The only move. The passive 13 ♔f3 ♔f7 14 ♔e3 ♖d5 leaves the white king cut off and unable to prevent the advance of the a-pawn.

13	...	♔f7
14	♖h6	♖c5
15	♖d6	♔e7
16	♖d4	♔e6
17	♖d8	♖d5
18	♖a8	♔d6
19	♔f6	♔c7
20	♔e6	♔b7
21	♖h8	

The transition into the pawn ending is hopeless: 21 ♔xd5 ♔xa8 22 ♔c5 ♔b7 23 ♔b5 ♔c7, and Black wins.

21	...	♖b5
22	♖h7+	♔b6
23	♖h8	a4

Black's laborious work has at last borne fruit – the a-pawn has advanced. But even here White should not have lost. One involuntarily recalls Tartakower's well-known witticism, that "all rook endings are drawn".

24	♖a8!	♖a5
25	♖b8+	♔c7
26	♖b2	a3
27	♖c2+	♔b6
28	♖a2	♔c6
29	♔f6	♔d6
30	♔g5	♔e7
31	♔g6	♔e6
32	♔g5?	

The decisive error. The simple 32 ♖e2+ would not have allowed the black king to cross the 5th rank.

32	...	♔f7!
33	♔h5	♔f6

34 ♔h4   ♖a8!

It was not yet too late to ruin everything: 34 ... ♔g6? 35 ♖xa3!, with stalemate.

35 ♔g3   ♖a4

0-1

MINOR PIECE ENDINGS

In this class of endings too there are subtle nuances, which may be noticed only by a true master, enabling him to breathe life into seemingly dreary positions, where many less skilled players would have given up the struggle.

Matulović-Vilela
Sombor 1978

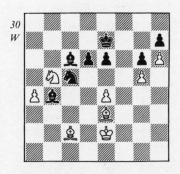

30
W

The kingside pawn formation suggests to us White's main combinational idea – the sacrifice of his bishop at g6.

1 e5   ♗xb5+

On 1 ... de White wins by 2 ♗xc5 ♗xc5 3 ♗xg6!.

2 ab   ♗c3

This bishop obviously intends to 'keep watch' over the white pawns along the a1-h8 diagonal. But White can prevent this.

3 ♗f4!   de

4 ♗d2   ♗d4

If Black exchanges bishops, White combines the threat to the g6 pawn with the advance of his passed b-pawn, and quickly puts his opponent in zugzwang – 4 ... ♗xd2 5 ♔xd2 ♔f7 6 ♔e3 followed by ♔e4 and the advance of the pawn. He wins even more quickly if the knight instead of the king goes to the defence of the kingside pawns: 5 ... ♘d7 6 ♗xg6! ♘f8 7 ♗xh7!.

5 ♗xg6!

White nevertheless makes this sacrifice!

5 ...   hg

6 h7   e4

7 ♗b4!

Black resigns – he cannot simultaneously stop both White's passed pawns: 7 ... ♔d6 8 b6 ♔c6 9 ♗xc5!.

And now a few examples where the decisive factor is the active placing of one side's minor pieces or pawns.

Rubinstein-Lasker
Moscow 1925

Black has a positional advantage – he has the more active pawn

31
B

formation on the queenside, and White's d-pawn is weak. See how brilliantly Lasker exploits his positional pluses to gain a deserved victory.

1	**...**	**a4!**
2	**ba**	

White has nothing else, since 2 b4 allows 2 ... ♘c4, and against 2 ♗a5 Lasker had prepared a brilliant reply – 2 ... ab! 3 ♗xb6 ♗g5!!.

2	**...**	**ba**
3	**♔f1**	

Activating his king is White's only chance. The knight ending after 3 ♗b4 ♗xb4 4 ab a3 5 ♘d2 a2 6 ♘b3 ♔f8 is hopeless for him.

3	**...**	**♗xa3**
4	**♔e2**	**♔f8**
5	**♔d3**	**♘d5**
6	**♗e1**	**♗d6**
7	**♔c4**	**♔e7**
8	**♘e5**	**♗xe5**
9	**de**	**♔d7**
10	**♗d2**	**h5!**
11	**♗c1**	

After 11 ♔b5 a3 12 ♗c1 ♘c3! the knight breaks through to the kingside pawns.

11	**...**	**♔c6**
12	**♗a3**	**♘b6+**
13	**♔d4**	**♔b5**
14	**♗f8**	**♘c4**
15	**♔c3**	**g6**
16	**f4**	**♘e3**
17	**♔d3**	**♘d5**

Now the inevitable ... h4 will break up White's pawn chain, and he is unable to prevent this. In the event of 16 h4 the black knight transfers to f5, when the pawns are doomed.

18	**♗a3**	**h4**
19	**gh**	**♘xf4+**
20	**♔e4**	**♘h5**

Of course, greediness such as 20 ... ♘xh3 does not lead to any good – 21 ♔f3 ♘g1+ 22 ♔f2 with a perpetual attack on the knight.

21	**♔f3**	

White's last hope is to break through with his king to the f7 pawn.

21	**...**	**♔c4**
22	**♗b2**	**♔b3**
23	**♗a1**	**a3**
24	**♔g4**	**♔c2**
25	**♔g5**	**♔d3!**

0-1

While the white king is winning the f7 pawn, Black has time to post his king at f5, when his knight acquires unrestricted freedom.

**Zatulovskaya-Chiburdanidze
Lvov 1977**

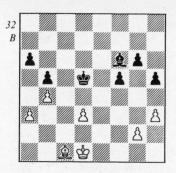

32
B

With material equal, there are very few pieces left on the board, which in itself suggests that a draw is imminent. But Black's position has some significant advantages: active pieces and a kingside pawn majority. And the white pawns fixed on black squares at a3 and b4 constitute an organic weakness.

The sum total of all these small pluses gives Black real winning chances. But the path to victory is highly tortuous. The realization of the advantage divides into several stages.

1	...	g5!
2	♔e2	g4
3	♔f2	♗e5
4	♔e2	f4
5	hg	hg

The first stage is completed, with Black's kingside pawns having successfully advanced.

| 6 | ♔f1 | ♔e6 |
| 7 | ♔e2 | ♔f5 |

| 8 | ♔f1 | ♗d4! |

An important finesse. Exploiting the fact that, in view of the threat of ... ♗b2, the white bishop is tied to c1, Black successfully carries out the next stage of her plan – improving the position of her king, while at the same time creating a passed pawn.

9	♔e2	♔e5
10	♔f1	f3
11	gf	gf
12	♗h6	♔d5
13	♗f8	♔e6
14	♔e1	♔e5
15	♔f1	♔f4
16	♗h6+	♔g4
17	♗f8	♗b2
18	♗c5	♗xa3

The a3 pawn has finally been won. Now the advance of Black's queenside pawns becomes decisive.

19	d4	♔f5
20	d5	a5
21	d6	♔e6
22	d7	♔xd7
23	♔f2	♗xb4

and **Black won**.

**Lerner-Godes
USSR 1979**

To win, Black has somehow to get at the h3 pawn – an extremely difficult task. The opposite coloured bishops suggest a draw. But the white knight at c8 has clearly been over-active, and is cut off from the rest of its pieces. Black exploits

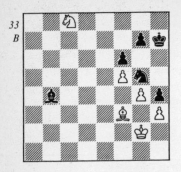

33
B

this factor to his great advantage.

| 1 | ... | ♗c5 |

White's knight has been 'hobbled' and his king is obliged to guard the h3 pawn, so that only his bishop has any scope to move.

2	♗d5	♔h6
3	♗g8	g6
4	fg	♔xg6
5	♗c4	♔g7
6	♗b3	

It would have been useful to restrict the black knight by 6 ♗d5!.

| 6 | ... | ♘e4 |
| 7 | ♗a4 | ♘d2!! |

Note how skilfully Black creates a zugzwang situation. The white king becomes a silent witness to the helplessness of his small army.

8	♗e8	♔h6
9	♗a4	♔g5
10	♗e8	♔f4
11	♗d7	♘c4
12	♔f1	♘e5
13	♗f5	♔e3
14	♔g2	♘f3
15	♔f1	♘d4

| 16 | ♗d7 | ♘e2 |
| 17 | g5 | |

Forced, since otherwise the h3 pawn cannot be defended.

17	...	fg
18	♗e6	♘d4
19	♗d5	♘f3
20	♗e6	♘e5
21	♗d5	♘d3
22	♗e6	♔f3

0-1

Kurajica-Karpov
Skopje 1976

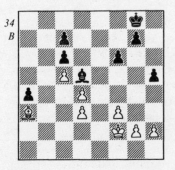

34
B

Black's passed pawn and much more active bishop give him a slight positional plus. But for a win this is clearly insufficient – White still has to go wrong . . .

| 1 | ... | h4! |
| 2 | g3 | |

Careful, but unconvincing. White could have created a fortress by 2 g4 and 3 h3.

| 2 | ... | ♔f7! |

White was evidently counting on 2 ... hg+ 3 hg, with an imminent draw. But it is all much more complicated. Black offers a pawn sacrifice, but in return gains the opportunity to activate his forces to the maximum.

3	♔e3	f5
4	♔f4	♔g6
5	♔e3?!	

This does not yet lose the game, but the marking time is a sure sign of White's unsureness in defence, otherwise he would have chosen 5 gh and if 5 ... ♔h5 6 ♔xf5. Such passiveness does not lead to any good.

5	...	♔h5
6	♗b4	g5

White's only real weakness is his h-pawn, and it is towards it that Black's plans are aimed. He now intends 7 ... f4+ with the possible sequel 8 gf g4! 9 fg+ ♔xg4 and 10 ... ♔h3.

7	♔f2	♗a2

Karpov undoubtedly realizes that the d3 pawn is best attacked from a6, but Black's 'futile' marking time with his bishop plays an important psychological role – it lulls the opponent's vigilance and provokes him into a burst of activity.

8	♗a3	♗b1
9	♔e2	♗a2
10	♗c1	♗e6
11	♔f2	♗c8
12	d5?	

The 'torture' mechanism has worked – White has nevertheless 'twitched'. And yet again the position was still drawn: 12 ♔e2! ♗a6 13 ♔e3 f4+ 14 gf g4 15 f5!, and the bishop at c1 comes in useful.

12	...	cd
13	d4	f4!
14	gf	

White can no longer set up a fortress – after 14 g4+ ♔g6 the black king breaks through via the queenside, while the white pawns at f3 and g4 require the constant attention of their king.

14	...	g4
15	♔g2	♗f5
16	♔f2	gf
17	♔xf3	♗e4+
18	♔f2	♔g4
19	♗b2	♔xf4
20	♗c1+	♔g4
21	♗b2	c6
22	♗c1	♔h3
23	♔g1	♗g6
24	♔h1	

This awkward move is White's only possibility. His bishop is forced to control the invasion square f4, and his king to defend the h2 pawn.

24	...	♗h5
25	♔g1	♗d1! *(35)*

In this position **White resigned**, a decision which is by no means premature – he is in zugzwang. For example: 26 ♔h1 ♔g4 27 ♔g2 ♔f5 28 ♔f2 ♔e4.

**Vaganian-Rashkovsky
Moscow 1981**

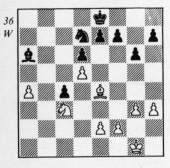

It may seem unfounded for White to play for a win in this ending. Yes, his passed pawn is more distant than his opponent's, but no other real pluses in the position are evident. However, there is a highly significant factor, as Vaganian shrewdly notices. Black's kingside has been abandoned by all his pieces, and in addition his pawns are on white squares (with a white-squared bishop!). Vaganian makes use of all these small pluses to carry out an original plan of a pawn squeeze of Black's kingside.

1	f4!	♚d8
2	h4	♚c7
3	a5!	

Play with the pawns in such endings is exceptionally difficult and committal. With his last move White essentially sacrifices his only passed pawn. But on winning it Black will spend a minimum of three tempi, and White advantageously uses this time to activate his king and strengthen the pawn blockade.

3	...	♘c5
4	♚f2	♘b3
5	g4	♚d8

The king is forced to retreat to the wing which it has left unattended. White threatens h4-h5-h6 and f4-f5, after which the h-pawn is unstoppable.

6	h5	♚e8

6 ... gh is bad: 7 g5!.

7	h6	♘xa5
8	f5	

White's threat is obvious – a double blow on g6, first with the pawn and then the bishop. The black king is forced to take up a passive position.

8	...	♚f8
9	g5	♘b3
10	♚e3	

Black is essentially playing without his king, a factor which is bound to prove decisive. But the path to victory is still lengthy.

10	...	♘c5
11	♗c2	♗c8

Black provokes a relieving of the pawn tension. Note that he could not have prevented f5-f6: 11 ... ♘d7 12 ♔d4 and then 13 ♗a4.

12	f6	♗h3
13	♗a4!	ef
14	gf	♘xa4

15 ♗c6 was threatened, after which the d6 pawn would have been doomed.

15	♘xa4	g5
16	♘c3	g4
17	♔f2!	

Note how subtly Vaganian plays this ending, as he puts his opponent in zugzwang. Black's forces are almost completely paralyzed.

17	...	♔e8
18	♘b5	♔d7
19	e4	

That wise man Rauzer was right – without this move White cannot win!

19	...	♔d8
20	♘xd6	c3
21	♘xf7+	♔c7
22	♘e5	g3+

A last spark of activity.

23	♔xg3	c2
24	♘d3	♗f1
25	♘c1	♔d7
26	e5	♗c4
27	d6	♗e6

28	♔f4

The apotheosis of White's deep and subtle strategy.

28	...	♔c6

1-0

A splendidly played ending by Vaganian, which will undoubtedly join the chess classics.

Ghinda-Ungureanu
Romania 1975

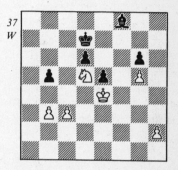

37
W

A typical position with a good knight against a bad bishop. Black's difficulties are also aggravated by the fact that he cannot go into the pawn ending – in this case White creates an outside passed pawn.

1	h4	♗g7

Let us convince ourselves that the pawn ending is indeed hopeless for Black: 1 ... ♗e7? 2 ♘xe7 ♔xe7 3 ♔d5 ♔d7 4 b4! ♔e7 5 c4 bc 6 ♔xc4 ♔e6 7 b5 d5+ 8 ♔b3 e4 9 b6 ♔d6 10 h5! gh 11 g6 and wins.

2	b4!	♗h8
3	c4!	bc

4	b5	♗g7
5	♘c3	

The knight vacates d5 for its king. Black has to prevent such activity by the opponent, but in doing so his king moves away from the passed b-pawn.

5	...	♔e6

5 ... ♗f8 is met by 6 ♔d5 ♗e7 7 ♔xc4 ♗d8 8 ♔d5 ♗b6 9 ♘e4, when White wins.

6	b6	♔d7
7	♔d5	e4!
8	♘b5!!	

A precise move! Now the appearance of white and black queens is inevitable, but White is the first to begin an attack, and this proves decisive.

8	...	c3
9	b7	c2
10	b8♕	c1♕
11	♕xd6+	♔c8
12	♕e6+	♔b8
13	♕b6+	♔c8
14	♘d6+	♔d7
15	♕b5+	

1-0

And to conclude this chapter – the struggle in two 'pure' knight endings.

Vasyukov-Timoshchenko
Volgodonsk 1981

White's positional advantage is obvious, but it has to be converted into a material one. The whole

38
W

question is which black pawn to eliminate – c5 or g5. Vasyukov finds the correct plan, and by precise manoeuvring deprives Black of any possibility of counterplay.

1	♘e4	♔e8
2	♔d6	

Knight opposition in a knight ending! The impulsive 2 ♘xg5 would have made White's task ultra-difficult after 2 ... ♘f2.

2	...	♔f8
3	♘xc5	♘f2
4	♘d7+	♔f7
5	♘e5+	

White has carried out the first part of his plan – his c-pawn has become passed, and the g4 pawn is defended by his knight. But the win is still far from easy. If the passed pawn is advanced with the support of the king, Black will give up his knight for it and his king will break through to the g4 pawn. Therefore White must at the same time also create threats against the g5 pawn, and to this aim he carries out a necessary regrouping.

5	...	♚f6
6	♚d5	♞d1
7	c5	♞c3+
8	♚c4	♞e4
9	♞d3!	

Have you managed to guess yet where the white knight is making for? If not, don't be upset, it is on a highly unusual route – aiming for h3.

9	...	♚e6
10	♚d4	♞f6
11	♞f2	♚e7
12	c6	♚e6

Watch out, a mine! After 12 ... ♚d6? 13 ♞e4+ the pawn ending is hopeless for Black.

13	♚c5	♚e7
14	♚b6	♚d6
15	♞h3!	

On this occasion too zugzwang comes to White's aid.

15	...	♞d5+
16	♚b7	♚e5
17	♞xg5	♚f4
18	♞h7!	

This knight is clearly intent on becoming a 'Trojan horse' – 18 ... ♚xg4 19 ♞f6+!.

| 18 | ... | ♞c3 |
| 19 | g5 | |

Only not 19 c7 because of 19 ... ♞b5 20 c8♛ ♞d6+.

| 19 | ... | ♚f5 |
| 20 | c7 | |

Now this is possible . . . **Black resigns.**

Barcza-Sanchez
Munich 1958

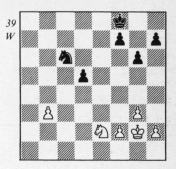

39 W

White has an outside passed pawn, but before using this trump he must co-ordinate the actions of his king and knight.

1 ♞c3!

'Urging on' the d-pawn to its doom: 1 ... d4? 2 ♞a2 ♚e7 3 ♚f3.

1	...	♞b4
2	♚f3	♚e7
3	♞b5!	♚d7
4	♚e3	♚c6
5	♞d4+	♚c5
6	h4!	

The first part of the plan has successfully been carried out – the passed b-pawn is tying down the opponent's forces, and now White intends to create threats on the kingside.

6	...	♚d6
7	g4!	♚c5
8	f4	♚d6
9	♞f3!	

The white knight is much more agile than its opponent.

9   ...   f6

9 ... h6 is bad, since after 10 h5 ♚c5 11 g5! White breaks through on the kingside.

10   ♘d4!   ♘a6

The black king can no longer return to c5, due to 11 ♘e6+ and 12 ♘f8.

11	♘c2	♚c5
12	♚d3	♘c7
13	b4+	♚b5
14	♚c3!	♚c6

Of course, Black cannot contemplate the hopeless pawn ending after 14 ... ♘e6 15 ♘d4+.

15	♘d4+	♚d6
16	♚d3!	

White is on the alert. The naive 16 ♚b3 is clearly refuted by 16 ... g5! 17 hg fg 18 fg ♚e5.

16	...	♘e8
17	f5!	

Threatening 18 fg hg 19 h5. Black is forced to exchange on f5.

17	...	gf
18	♘xf5+	♚e5
19	b5	♘c7
20	b6	♘a6
21	♚e3	♘c5

21 ... h5 is rather strongly met by 22 ♚f3!.

22	h5!	♘b7
23	♘d4	♚d6
24	♘b3!	♚c6
25	♚d4!	

This change of guard on the blockade square is a typical procedure in such endings.

25	...	♚d6
26	♘c1!	♘d8
27	♘d3	♘c6+

White also wins after 27 ... ♘e6+ 28 ♚e3 ♚c6 29 ♘b4+.

28	♚e3	♘e7
29	♘b4	h6
30	♚d4	f5
31	g5!	

Precisely calculated: 31 ... hg 32 b7 ♚c7 33 ♘xd5+ ♘xd5 34 ♚xd5 g4 35 ♚d4!.

31	...	f4
32	gh	♘f5+
33	♚d3	♘xh6
34	♘xd5	

1-0

An instructive ending, conducted by White with great subtlety from beginning to end.

2 Exploiting a Small Material Advantage

The aim of a game of chess is to give mate to the opponent's king. I beg the reader's forgiveness for repeating this truism. But what in fact happens at the chess board when a game between two fairly proficient players ends in victory for one of the sides? Usually, one of the players has a positional advantage of decisive proportions. It follows that the most universal way of realizing a small material advantage is to transform it into a decisive positional advantage. This is quite sufficient to win.

Here we will examine some examples from practical games, in which the advantage (material) of one of the sides is so insignificant (for example, the activity of the opponent's pieces almost compensates for him being a pawn down), that many players would be reconciled to a draw. Many, only not true masters! If there is even the slightest chance, although it may involve colossal difficulties – battle on! Only, it is important not to cling on to an insignificant material advantage, but to play actively, and fight to the end on every square of the chess board. And this craving for a battle and for victory will be rewarded!

We will first examine some endings which demonstrate . . . the might of the king.

KINGS CAN DO ANYTHING!

**Polgar-Barcza
Hungary 1969**

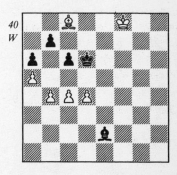

40
W

The white king appears to be right out of it, but this impression is deceptive. In general, an invasion by the king from the rear can often prove decisive in such endings.

One gains the impression that on the 7th and 8th ranks the king in the endgame receives an additional supply of activity and strength. It is important always to remember this!

    1   ♔e8!

An extra pawn is not an end in itself. The chief motto is activity! Both 1 c5+ ♔c7 and 1 ♗xb7 ♗xc4 lead to an inevitable draw.

    1   ...   ♗xc4

Here 1 ... ♔c7 no longer helps. White plays 2 ♗e6, and after 2 ... ♔d6 3 ♗f7 ♔c7 4 ♔e7 the passed d-pawn decides the game.

    2   ♔d8   ♔d5
    3   ♗xb7   ♔xd4
    4   ♗xc6   ♔c3
    5   ♔c7!

Of course, not 5 b5? ♗xb5! 6 ♗xb5 ♔b4!, when the a-pawn is not destined to become a queen.

    5   ...   ♔xb4
    6   ♔b6   ♗e6
    7   ♗b7

The a6 pawn has to be captured by the bishop – the king is controlling the key c5 square.

    7   ...   ♗d7
    8   ♗xa6   ♗h3
    9   ♗b5   ♗c8
    10   ♗c6
                        1-0

The goal is achieved – Black is in zugzwang. A highly instructive and interesting ending.

Lputyan-Lanka
Sevastopol 1982

41
W

The unfortunate placing of the white pawn chain on squares of the same colour as the bishops is compensated by the activity of his king and knight, and also by the weakness of the black b-pawn. It is for this pawn that the white knight now aims, diverting the opponent's bishop from a possible invasion on f1.

    1   ♘e6   ♔c3

After 1 ... ♗d7 2 ♘d8 h3 3 gh ♗xh3 4 ♘xb7 ♗d7! 5 ♘xd6 h4 6 ♗d3 it is difficult for Black to strengthen his position.

    2   ♘d8   ♗a4!

Transposing into a knight ending is Black's best practical chance. 2 ... ♗b5 is much weaker, after which it is Black who is in danger of losing: 3 ♘xb7 ♗f1 4 ♘xd6 ♗xg2 5 ♘f5! h3 6 d6 ♔c8 7 ♔c6 h2 8 d7+ ♔d8 9 ♘d6.

    3   ♗d3!

Let us satisfy ourselves that the

knight ending is hopeless for White: 3 ♗xa4? ♘xa4+ 4 ♔b5 ♘c3+ 5 ♔b6 ♘xd5+!! 6 ed e4.

3	...	♗d7
4	♘c6+!!	

A brilliant solution! Black is obliged to accept the piece sacrifice, and the c-pawn becomes extremely dangerous.

4	...	bc
5	dc	♘a4+!
6	♔b5	♗e8
7	♔xa4	♗xc6+
8	♔b4	

The tactical skirmish has concluded in a quite peaceful ending, in which only a certain accuracy is required of White to attain a draw.

8	...	♔c7
9	a4	

This does not lose the game, but 9 ♗c4 was more circumspect.

9	...	d5
10	ed	♗xd5
11	♗f5	

11 ... h3 was threatened.

11	...	♔d6
12	a5	♔c6
13	a6?? (42)	

This last move by White is a fatal mistake, although its cause is not hard to understand. By diverting the black king with his passed pawn, White hopes to break through with his king to the e5 pawn. This outwardly quite logical plan unexpectedly meets

with a study-like refutation. The a-pawn should not have been given up.

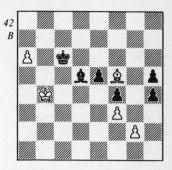

13	...	♔b6
14	a7	♗b7!
15	♗h3	

15 ♔c4 was rather stronger.

15	...	♔xa7
16	♔c5	♔b8!!

The wise king! Now Black's original idea becomes clear. White's planned 17 ♔d6 is decisively met by 17 ... e4! 18 fe ♗c8, with the inevitable exchange of bishops and the breakthrough of one of Black's kingside pawns.

17	♗e6	♔c7
18	♗f5	♗c6
19	♗e6	♗b7
20	♗f5	e4!
21	♔d4	

Forced. 21 fe loses to 21 ... ♗c8.

21	...	e3
22	♔d3	♗a6+
23	♔c2	♗e2
24	♗e6	♔d6
25	♗c8	♔e5

Without his king Black cannot manage . . .

26	♗d7	♔d4
27	♗f5	♔e5
28	♗d7	♗f1
29	♗h3	♗c4
30	♗d7	♗e6
31	♗e8	♗c4
32	♗d7	♔f6
33	♔d1	♗e6
34	♗e8	♔g5

White resigns. He is unable to prevent the decisive invasion of the black king.

A STUDY-LIKE MOVE

In the following game fragments the outcome is decided by study-like moves, of which even study composers might be envious.

**Simagin-Bronstein
Moscow 1947**

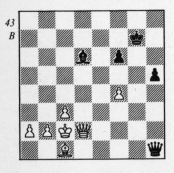

In spite of being two pawns down, Black has good drawing

chances after the possible 1 ... ♛e4+. But Bronstein decides to sacrifice his bishop with the aim of exploiting the strength of his passed h-pawn. An undoubtedly very interesting idea, the incorrectness of which is not at all easy to demonstrate.

1	...	h4?!
2	♛xd6	♛g2+
3	♔b3	h3

It was for this position that Black was aiming. Nothing can prevent the h-pawn from promoting to a queen. However, White can give perpetual check . . .

4	♛d7+	♔g8

The king cannot go to g6: 4 ... ♔g6? 5 f5+ ♔h5 6 ♗f4!

5	f5	h2
6	♗g5!!	

Where are you, study composers? This idea was not foreseen even by Bronstein with his computer brain! The bishop moves into a double attack, Black can obtain a new queen, but in every case his future is cheerless.

6	...	h1♛

6 ... fg is met by 7 f6!, and 6 ... ♛xg5 by 7 ♛c8+ and 8 ♛c7+.

7	♛e8+	♔g7
8	♛g6+	♔f8
9	♛xf6+	♔g8
10	♛d8+!	♔g7
11	♛e7+	♔g8
12	♛e8+	

1-0

Möhring-Kaikamdzhozhov
Zamardy 1978

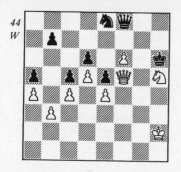

44
W

Formally White is a pawn up, which makes the path that he chooses in search of victory even more cautious.

| 1 | f7! | ♘g7 |
| 2 | ♕f6+!! | |

White's original plan becomes obvious – he sacrifices his knight, but puts his opponent's pieces in zugzwang.

| 2 | ... | ♔xh5 |
| 3 | ♔h3 | ♘e8 |

Black also fails to save the game by 3 ... ♕c8+ 4 ♔g2! ♕f8 5 ♔g3.

| 4 | ♕f5+! | ♔h6 |
| 5 | ♕e6+ | ♔h7 |

It looks as though Black could have saved himself here by 5 ... ♔g7, but then the spectacular 6 fe♘+! decides matters.

6	fe♕	♕f3+
7	♔h4	♕f2+
8	♔h5	♕h2+

Surely all White's efforts haven't been in vain, and Black can draw by perpetual check?

| 9 | ♕h3!! | |

Brilliant! White returns his extra queen, but his king escapes from the annoying checks.

9	...	♕xh3+
10	♔g5	♕g3+
11	♔f6	♕f3+
12	♔e7	♕xb3

Or 12 ... ♕xe4 13 ♔xd6 followed by ♕xe5.

13	♕h5+	♔g7
14	♕g4+!	
	1-0	

Milenković-Stankov
Yugoslavia 1970

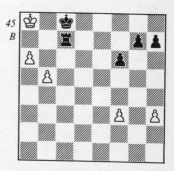

45
B

The experienced reader is unlikely to be surprised at the fact that in this position the stronger side's advantage is deemed to be minimal. We should not be deluded by Black's extra rook – White's connected passed pawns are very strong. Black's pawn majority on the kingside is the only clue to the solution. Black must first of all stop the opponent's pawns at any cost, and only then create his own passed pawn. He does this in a highly spectacular way.

| 1 | ... | ♖c6!! |

The white king is essentially stalemated in the corner, and this factor decides the game.

| 2 | bc |

Or 2 ♔a7 ♔c7!

2	...	g5!
3	a7	f5
4	c7	

White has stalemated himself – a last, but unrealizable saving chance.

4	...	f4!
5	h4	g4
6	h5	h6!

0-1

The black f-pawn queens first and inflicts a deadly blow along the h1-a8 diagonal.

Ubilava-Vitolinš
Yurmala 1977

46
W

We should not be captivated by White's extra pawn. Black is threatening ... d3, and White is obliged to play very determinedly. And he succeeds in finding the latent preconditions for . . . a mating attack!

| 1 | b4+ | ♔xb4 |
| 2 | ♔d5 | |

Do you sense how cramped it is now becoming for the black king on the edge of the board?

| 2 | ... | ♖e3 |

No better is 2 ... d3 3 ♘xd3+ ♔b5 4 ♖f4! ♗a1 5 ♖b4+ ♔a5 6 ♖b3 ♖xa2 7 ♔c6, and White mates.

| 3 | ♖f4 | ♔b5 |

Black appears to be able to save the game by 3 ... ♔c3, but here too White wins prettily: 4 f6 d3 5 f7 ♖xe5+ 6 ♔xe5 ♔c2+ 7 ♔e6 d2 8 f8♕ d1♕ 9 ♕f5+, or 6 ... d2 7 f8♕ d1♕ 8 ♕c5+ ♔d3 9 ♔e6 ♕e2+ 10 ♔f7!

| 4 | ♘c6!! | |

White is all ready for his mating attack: 4 ... d3 5 ♖b4+ ♔a6 6 ♔c5!

4	...	♖e2
5	f6	d3
6	f7	

As long as c2 is free for the black rook, mate cannot be given, so White must wait.

| 6 | ... | d2 |

But now the appropriate moment has arrived . . .

| 7 | ♖b4+ | ♔a6 |

8   ♔c5!
1-0

Sherwin-Gufeld
Helsinki 1961

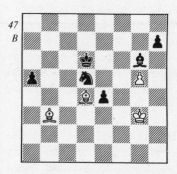

Black is two pawns up, but how is he to set them in motion? The white pieces are keeping a very sharp eye on them.

Let us try working out a test variation: 1 ... e3 2 ♗xd5 ♔xd5 3 ♗xe3 a4 4 ♗c1 ♔c4 5 ♔f3 ♔b3 6 ♔e2 a3 7 ♗f4 a2 8 ♗e5 ♔c2 and then 9 ... ♔b1, winning the bishop and the game. So, shall we be off?

But for what reason is this 'cunning' game of chess so wonderful? for its latent, inexhaustible possibilities! And so, let us begin again: 1 ... e3 2 ♗xd5 ♔xd5, and here (miraculously!) White has a truly study-like move which saves the game – not the plausible capture of the pawn (3 ♗xe3?), but 3 ♗b6!! *(48)*.

The bishop 'urges on' the a-pawn – move forward, my dear!

But in doing so a highly important tempo is gained for the white king.

After 3 ... a4 4 ♔f3 a3 5 ♔xe3 ♔c4 6 ♗d4! ♔b3 7 ♔d2 the game is a draw: White's king reaches d2 just in time (7 ... ♔a2 8 ♔c1). Hence the conclusion: 1 ... e3? is a mistake, throwing away the win. But the winning idea has been found, it is important merely to formulate it in the appropriate way.

The game in fact continued:

1	...	♗h5
2	♔f2	♔e6
3	♔g3	♗e2!
4	♔h4	♔d6
5	♔g3	♗b5!
6	♗c2	♗d3
7	♗b3	e3!

Now this sacrifice succeeds.

8	♗xd5	♔xd5
9	♗xe3	

Here 9 ♗b6 no longer works: 9 ... a4 10 ♔f3 e2.

9	...	a4
10	♗c1	♔c4

11	♔f2	♚b3
12	♗f4	a3
13	♔e3	a2
14	♗e5	♚c2
15	♔f4	♗g6
16	♗d4	♚b1
	0-1	

MAKE WAY FOR HIS MAJESTY THE PAWN!

It is now time to devote our attention to pawns, the role of which grows immeasurably in the concluding stage of the game.

Shirazi-Vasyukov
India 1978

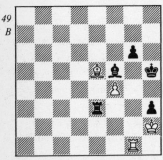

The h-pawn on its own is not able to queen – here a pair of connected passed pawns is needed. This means that an opportunity for advancing the g-pawn must be found. And Black finds it.

1	...	♖e2+
2	♔g3	g5!
3	♔f3	h2!
4	♖a1	

The only move. White loses quickly after 4 ♖xg5+ ♚h4 or 4 ♖h1 ♗e4+ 5 ♔xe2 ♗xh1 6 fg ♗f3+!

| 4 | ... | g4+! |

A striking solution! So as to obtain two connected passed pawns, Black sacrifices a whole rook! White cannot decline the sacrifice: 5 ♔g3 ♗e4.

5	♔xe2	g3
6	♔f3	♚h4
7	♗d4	♚h3

In spite of his extra rook, White is helpless.

| 8 | ♗f2 | g2! |
| | 0-1 | |

Passerotti-Joksic
Banja Luka 1978

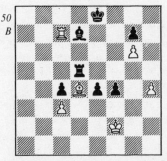

White's only hope of saving the game is his g-pawn, but it is never in fact able to move. By several spectacular blows Black concludes the game.

| 1 | ... | e3+ |
| 2 | ♔f3 | |

After 2 ♔g2 Black wins very

prettily: 2 ... ♖xd4 3 cd ♗h3+!! 4
♔g1 f3, while on 2 ♔e2 he has the
decisive 2 ... ♗g4+ 3 ♔e1 ♖xd4
4 cd f3.

2 ... ♖xd4!

This universal exchange sacrifice
is constantly in the air.

3 cd ♗g4+!

Yet another sacrifice is laid on
the altar of victory!

4 ♔xf4

What else? 4 ♔xg4 e2 5 ♖c5
e1♕ 6 ♖e5+ ♕xe5 7 de c3 is
hopeless for White, and Black's
task is even easier after 4 ♔g2 f3+
5 ♔g3 f2.

4 ... e2!

0-1

Gufeld-Smyslov
Riga 1975

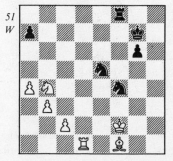

51
W

In spite of the limited material,
the position is exceptionally complicated. For the moment White's
extra pawn is not making itself felt
at all, whereas his king may come
under dangerous threats. Only
after White has safeguarded his

monarch can he set about realizing
his queenside pawn majority.

1	♔e3!	♘g4+
2	♔d2	g5
3	♘c6	♘f2
4	♖e1	g4
5	b4	g3
6	b5	

Exploiting the fact that for the
moment Black cannot play 6 ... g2
due to 7 ♗xg2 ♘xg2 8 ♖g1, White
skilfully creates a connected pair
of passed pawns.

6	...	♖f5!
7	c4!	

The hasty 7 a5? would have
allowed Black to defend: 7 ... g2 8
♗xg2 ♖xb5!

| 7 | ... | g2 |

It was hard to resist the
temptation to win a piece, but 7 ...
♘g4 came into consideration.

8	♗xg2	♘xg2
9	♖e7+	♔f6
10	a5!	

Black's extra piece by no means
guarantees him a quiet life – the
white pawns are too dangerous.

10	...	♖f4
11	c5!	

Much stronger than 11 b6 ab 12
ab ♘e4+.

11	...	♘e4+
12	♖xe4	♖xe4
13	b6!	

In such a situation time is worth
its weight in gold.

| 13 | ... | ♖e8 |

13 ... ab also does not help: 14 cb! ♘e3 15 b7 ♖e8 16 a6 ♘c4+ 17 ♔d3 ♘d6 18 b8♕ ♖xb8 19 ♘xb8 – the a-pawn cannot be stopped. In the endgame pawns endeavour to capture not towards the centre, but away from it. The more distant, the more dangerous they are.

14 ♘xa7!

A cool and precise decision. Only a draw results from 14 b7 ♔e6 15 b8♕ ♖xb8 16 ♘xb8 ♔d5.

14 ... ♘e3

The black pieces are too dis-united.

15 a6 ♘c4+

After 15 ... ♔e6 16 ♘c8!! the white pawns would have shown themselves in their full glory.

16	♔c3	♘e5
17	b7	♔e6
18	c6	♔d5
19	c7	

1-0

Leybov-Kotkov
Chelyabinsk 1954

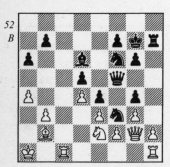

52
B

How should this position be assessed? White is the exchange up, but he is manifestly lacking in oxygen. Black finds an original way to win. First he has to obtain a new square of invasion into the enemy position for his minor pieces.

1	...	♘d2
2	♔a2	♕f3!
3	♕xf3	ef
4	♘c3	♘fe4
5	♘xe4	♘xe4
6	♖c2	

At first sight White appears to have defended successfully. But this is by no means so. Black's far-advanced pawns persistently demand to have their say!

6 ... ♘xf2!

7 ♖xf2 ♗xg3

At the present moment White is a rook up. But 8 ♖c2 is met by another sacrifice – 8 ... ♖xh2!!, and after 9 ♖cxh2 ♗xh2 10 ♖xh2 g3 one of the black pawns is bound to queen.

8 hg ♖xh1

Now the g3 pawn falls, and the unwieldy bishop is unable to arrive in time to help.

9	♗c3	♖g1
10	♔a3	♖xg3
11	♔b4	♖h3!

Threatening ... g3.

| 12 | ♖f1 | g3 |
| 13 | ♗e1 | |

The ending arising after 13

♖xf3 g2 14 ♖xh3 g1♛ is quite hopeless for White.

13	...	g2
14	♖g1	g5!

Decisive reinforcements!

15	♗f2	g4
16	e4	g3
17	♗e3	♖h1
18	ed	♖xg1
19	♗xg1	f2

0-1

The pawn avalanche has swept away everything in its path.

Commons-Mednis
Houston 1974

53
B

It is well known that a rook together with a pair of connected pawns wins against a rook. Very often it does not require the help of its king. In this unusual example the rook succeeds in pushing through one of its pawns to the queening square, although Black's passed pawns are not only not connected, but are even at a respectable distance from each other.

1	...	a4!
2	g4!	

White is obliged to play actively.

| 2 | ... | e3! |

A splendid reply! Black sacrifices a pawn, to divert the white king from the defence of the c-pawn.

| 3 | ♖a2! | |

White too rises to the occasion. 3 ♔xe3 would have lost to 3 ... fg 4 ♔d4 ♖g5!

| 3 | ... | f4! |

The a-pawn is sacrificed, but a pawn pair is acquired.

| 4 | ♖xa4 | |

The pawn pair is usually 'dragged' by the rook, which clears the way for it, so what now?

| 4 | ... | ♖e5! |

A highly elegant solution to the problem. White is obliged to accept the rook sacrifice.

| 5 | ♔xe5 | e2! |

This is stronger than 5 ... f3 6 ♖a3, when White can still offer some resistance.

6	♔xf4	e1♛
7	♔g5	h4!

Battling against a lone queen would still be possible, but here Black has another queen, as yet unborn – the h-pawn.

0-1

Matushkin-Shumilov
Correspondence 1974

54
B

The material advantage is with White, but in the given position this factor is not of great significance – Black's pair of connected passed pawns is highly dangerous. Even so, it is hard to believe that White cannot save the game.

1	...	g2+
2	♔e1	♗d2+!!

The reader will already have noticed how ready bishops are to sacrifice themselves. And here too a bishop diverts the enemy king away from the key squares. White cannot play 3 ♔d1 because of 3 ... ♘d4!, and so he is obliged to accept the sacrifice.

3	♔xd2	♘d4!
4	♘xd4	

White also fails to save the game by 4 ♗xd4 ed 5 ♘xd4 f2!

4	...	g1♕
5	♘b5	

Equally after 5 ♘xf3 ♕xa7 6 ♗e2 ♔g4! White's position cannot be held.

5	...	♕a1!

Accuracy to the end. 5 ... f2 6 ♘xc7 could have led to unpleasant complications.

6	♘xc7

On 6 ♗b7 Black has the decisive 6 ... ♕b2+.

6	...	♕a5+
	0-1	

In the variation 7 ♔e3 ♕xc7 8 ♗b7 ♕a5 9 ♗b8 ♕c3+ 10 ♔f2 ♕d3 the white king ends up in a mating net.

Makarichev-Averbakh
Lvov 1973

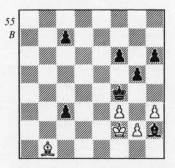

55
B

Black's material advantage has a definite, but not decisive importance. The main factor in this example is the activity of Black's pieces – in the end it is this that brings him victory.

1	...	♗g1+!
2	♔e2	

The bishop cannot be taken, since the black king would break through to the c3 pawn, and it would all be over.

2	...	♔g3
3	♔f1	♗f2

Now White has only bishop moves.

4	♗c2	f5!

A pawn sacrifice with the aim of luring the bishop to f5 and gaining a decisive tempo by 5 ... ♔f4.

5	♗b1	f4

What is Black doing? A little later, and his original plan will become clear.

6	♗g6	♗e3
7	♗c2	h5
8	♗f5	c5
9	♗g6	h4! *(56)*

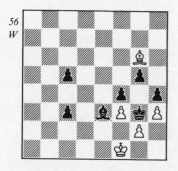

56
W

White has the white squares, and Black the black.

10	♗f5	g4!

Here it is, the desired breakthrough!

11	hg	

If 11 fg f3 12 gf ♔xh3 13 g5+ ♔g3 14 g6 ♗d4, and the curtain can be lowered.

11	...	h3
12	gh	♔xf3

13	g5	♔g3
14	g6	♗d4
15	h4	f3
16	h5	♗g7
17	♔e1	f2+

White resigned, and don't imagine that this is too soon. Of course, the f-pawn is not going to queen; this role has been prepared for the c5 pawn.

FROM THE CHESS CLASSICS

These fragments from games by outstanding players of various times show us examples of very fine technique.

Capablanca-Alekhine
World Championship Match
29th game Buenos Aires 1927

57
W

White's extra pawn and more active pieces are not sufficient for a win. He must create a passed pawn, or else break up the black king's pawn screen by a knight sacrifice.

1 ♘e5!

Unequivocally aiming at the g6 pawn.

1	...	♝g7
2	♕a8+	♚h7
3	♘f3	♝f6

White's knight is restricted, but there is also his extra pawn . . .

4	♕a6	♚g7
5	♕d3	♕b7
6	e4	♕c6
7	h3!	

Note this characteristic detail of Capablanca's endgame play – he is not in a hurry to take active measures, but first he improves his position to the maximum and restricts the opponent's possible counterplay.

7	...	♕c7
8	d5	ed
9	ed	

Having created a passed pawn, White is now very close to a win, but Alekhine finds a wonderful defensive resource, unexpectedly offering the exchange of queens.

9	...	♕c3!
10	♕xc3	♝xc3
11	♚f1!	♚f6
12	♚e2	♝b4!
13	♘d4!	

Black was intending after 13 ... ♝c5 not to allow the knight to go to c6.

13	...	♝c5
14	♘c6	♚f5
15	♚f3!	

The routine 15 f3 would have made the draw a reality: 15 ... ♝d6 16 g4+ hg 17 hg+ ♚f4.

15	...	♚f6
16	g4	hg+
17	hg	♚g5?

For an instant the f7 pawn is undefended, and White can advantageously exploit this factor. 17 ... ♝d6 was safer, retaining drawing chances.

| 18 | ♘e5 | ♝d4? |

18 ... ♝a3 19 ♘xf7+ ♚f6 should have been played, after which the knight would not have been so comfortably placed.

| 19 | ♘xf7+ | ♚f6 |
| 20 | ♘d8! | ♝b6 |

Had Black's bishop been at a3, 20 ... ♚e5 would now have been possible.

| 21 | ♘c6 | ♝c5 |

The familiar position has again arisen, but now without the f7 pawn – "a mysterious disappearance" . . .

22	♚f4	♝xf2
23	g5+	♚f7
24	♘e5+	♚e7
25	♘xg6	♚d6
26	♚e4	♝g3
27	♘f4	♚e7
28	♚e5	♝e1
29	d6+	♚d7
30	g6	♝b4
31	♚d5!	

But not 31 g7? ♝c3+.

| 31 | ... | ♚e8 |

32 d7+
1-0

The triumph of centralization – this is a factor that we frequently encounter, when playing through games by the stars from the past.

Rubinstein-Schlechter
Berlin 1913

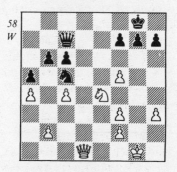

58
W

White is a pawn up, but this is one of the set of tripled (!) pawns on the f-file. However, on a careful examination of the position we see that White controls the d-file, the f5 pawn may be able to act as a battering-ram, and also at the moment Black's back rank is weak. Now follow with what virtuosity Rubinstein exploits these as yet imperceptible pluses, and sharply alters the picture of the battle by activating his pieces.

1 ♕d4!

Centralization is more important than a pawn, especially a wing pawn. Reckoning that his position is sound enough, Black accepts

the sacrifice, but 1 ... ♘d7 was more circumspect.

1 ... ♘xa4
2 f6 ♘c5

The exchange of knights is the only possibility of weakening the onslaught of the white pieces.

3 ♘xc5 bc
4 ♕g4 g6
5 ♕g3!

After keenly assessing the resulting pawn ending, White offers the exchange of queens. Black is forced to avoid the exchange, but in doing so he concedes the important e5 square.

5 ... ♕d8
6 ♕e5 a4
7 h4 h6

Black tries to safeguard his king – a sad necessity.

8 ♔g2 ♕c8
9 ♔g3 ♕d8
10 ♔g2 ♕c8

White gains time on the clock before the control.

11 ♕xc5 ♕e6
12 ♕e7! ♕c8
13 c5

Black is essentially in zugzwang.

13 ... g5

A desperate attempt to free himself, but even it fails. Note that there was also no sense in Black waiting: after 13 ... ♕a8 14 ♕d7 White throws forward his f3 pawn, breaking up the enemy king's pawn cover. Even tripled pawns can prove very useful!

14	hg	hg
15	♕e3	♛e6
16	♕xg5+	♚f8
17	♕g7+	♚e8
18	♕g8+	♚d7
19	♕g4!	♚e8
20	♕xe6+	fe
21	♚g3	♚f7
22	♚f4	♚xf6
23	♚e4	

0-1

Let us now return to the present time, and see how precisely Karpov realizes an insignificant material advantage. We have already had the opportunity to observe his virtuoso play in endings with opposite-coloured bishops, which have the hardly deserved reputation of being hopelessly drawn. Here is another example.

Karpov-Portisch
Milan 1975

White's advantage results not so much from his extra pawn, as from . . . the presence of opposite-coloured bishops. The point is that Black's pawns are mainly on black squares, which means that they can become a convenient target for the opponent. With fine technique, Karpov exploits the advantage of his position.

1	♚d3	h5
2	b5!	hg
3	fg	♖c8
4	♖a4!	

The black pawns will not 'run away' . . .

4	...	♝e6
5	g5	f5

This attempt to lift the blockade is the only chance of saving the game. 5 ... fg 6 hg ♚f7 does not help due to 7 ♝d4, when the b6 pawn falls.

6	ef	♝xf5+
7	♚d4	♚f7
8	♝b4	♚e6
9	♖a6	♖b8
10	h5	♝g4
11	h6	gh
12	gh	♝f5
13	♝d2!	

The h-pawn diverts Black's bishop, his rook is forced to guard the b6 pawn, and his king the d6 pawn. A thankless task faces the black pieces!

13	...	♖g8!
14	♝f4!	

No counterplay!

14	...	♖b8
15	♖a7	♔f6
16	♖g7	♗e6
17	♖c7	

For the moment the d-pawn is 'poisoned' – 17 ♗xd6 ♖d8.

17	...	♖h8
18	♖c6	

The rook has performed splendidly, and is ready to reap a rich harvest.

18	...	♖g8
19	♖xd6	♔f5
20	♖xb6	♖g4
21	♖xe6!	

Pretty and convincing!

21	...	♔xe6
22	♔e4	♖g1
23	b6	

1-0

THE KNIGHT SHOWS ITS SKILL

One can find many instructive examples in endings, where knights demonstrate their capabilities in the chess arena.

Portisch-Barcza
Hungary 1969 *(60)*

Knight endings can often be assessed as follows: it is sufficient mentally to remove the knights from the board and assess the resulting pawn ending. If it is won, the presence of the knights will merely make the realization of the

advantage slightly more difficult, but the principles will remain unchanged. If there were no knights here, White would win easily by setting up a passed pawn on the kingside.

1	f5+!	gf

White wins prettily after 1 ... ♔f7 – 2 g5! gf 3 ♔e5 ♔g6 4 h4.

2	gh	♔f6
3	♘d5+	

Otherwise Black transfers his knight to c7. Now interesting tempo play commences.

3	...	♔g5
4	♔e5!	♔xh5
5	♔e6!	f4
6	♔d7	

Not 6 ♘xf4+ ♔g5 7 ♘d5 ♘g7+ 8 ♔d7 ♘f5! when the black knight gets to the b5 pawn in time.

6	...	♘g7
7	♘xb6	♘f5
8	♘c4	♘d4
9	b6	♘b3
10	♔d6!	f3
11	b7	f2

12	♘e3	♞a5
13	b8♕	♞c4+
14	♔e6	♞xe3
15	♕e5+	

1-0

Mikhail Tseitlin-Szymczak

61
B

In this position there is much for both White and Black to consider. The limited material and the rather 'one-sided' nature of the play should be a sure drawing guide for Black. But how should he now play: bring up his knight, or deprive the opponent of the possibility of h6, which will restrict his king still further? A difficult question, to which it is not at all easy to give an answer. I fancy that the h-pawn should not have been advanced, when it would have been more difficult for White to create a passed pawn. At any rate, the possibility of stale-mating ideas would have been increased with the pawn at h7. Self-restricting play is yet another

problem in endings.

1	...	h6+?!
2	♔f4	♞d4
3	♘f3	♞e2+

If 3 ... ♞xf3 White wins by 4 gf!

4	♔f5	♞g3+
5	♔g4	♞e4
6	♔f4	♞f6
7	g4	

White has carried out the first part of his plan – his pawn has reached g4, but during this time Black too has managed to transfer his knight to the aid of his king.

7	...	♞d5+
8	♔e4	♞f6+
9	♔f5	♞d5
10	♘d4	♞e3+
11	♔f4	♞c4

Black can no longer continue his 'shuttle' play: after 11 ... ♞d5+? 12 ♔e5 ♞e3 13 ♘f5+ ♞xf5 14 gf White wins.

12	♘f5+	♔h7
13	♔e4	

White's king is aiming for f6, and Black is unable to prevent this. This is the result of ... h6 and the passive ... ♔h7 which was consequently forced.

13	...	♞d2+
14	♔e5	♞f3+
15	♔f6	♞h2
16	♘e3	♞f3
17	♘c4!	♞g5

Forced, since 17 ... ♞h2 is met by 18 ♘e5, when Black runs out of useful moves. Note this arrangement of the knights – at h2 and e5.

18 ♘d2!

And here is the mirror image! How a bishop 'cuts off' a knight – with an interval of two squares along a rank or file – is easy to remember, but how the knight does this is highly unusual and instructive – with an interval of two squares along a diagonal!

18	...	♘h3
19	♘e4	♘f4
20	♔f7	♔h8

Any knight move is decisively met by 21 ♘f6+ and 22 ♔g6.

21	♘f6	♘d3
22	♔g6	♘e5+
23	♔xh6	

and White won.

**Byelov-Mark Tseitlin
USSR 1979**

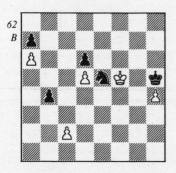

62
B

Despite the fact that White has only a pawn for a piece, the position is very complicated.

The white king is highly active, and the loss of the d6 pawn is an unpleasant threat for Black. The far-advanced a6 pawn should also not be forgotten. If it weren't for Black's b-pawn, he would be faced with a difficult defence. But it is there, and it is on this pawn that Tseitlin pins his ambitious hopes.

Even so, the fate of the game is decided not by the b-pawn, which promotes to a queen, but the a7 pawn. What's more, this silent and modest observer, fixed in its initial position, does not in fact move from its post.

1	...	♘d3!
2	♔e6	♘e1
3	♔xd6	♘xc2
4	♔c5	b3

Black will queen first, but will this give him winning chances?

5 d6 ♘d4!!

A splendid resource. The hasty 5 ... b2 6 d7 b1♕ 7 d8♕ with the threat of mate at g5 would have allowed White to save the game, but now on 6 ♔xd4 Black wins easily: 6 ... b2 7 d7 b1♕ 8 d8♕ ♕d1+.

6 ♔d5!

White defends cleverly – the enemy knight screens his king against a deadly check from below.

6	...	b2
7	d7	b1♕
8	d8♕	♕a2+!

It is an amazing combination of pieces, is queen and knight. In its ability to 'mine' the opponent's king position it has no equals. It is now clear that, due to the knight fork, the white king cannot go either to e5 or c5, while after 9 ♔e4 ♕g2+ 10 ♔d3 ♕c2+ 11 ♔e3 ♕e2+ White inevitably loses his queen. There only remains the move in the game.

9	♔d6	♕xa6+
10	♔d5	♕a2+
11	♔d6	♕e6+
12	♔c5	♕e5+
13	♕d5	

13 ♔c4 also fails to draw, due to 13 ... ♕c5+! 14 ♔xc5 ♘e6+ 15 ♔b5 ♘xd8 16 ♔a6 ♘c6 followed by the victorious advance of the a-pawn.

13	...	♘e6+
14	♔c4	♕xd5+
15	♔xd5	♘c7+
16	♔c6	♔xh4

0-1

If we recall the initial position and follow the entire subsequent 'route' of the black knight, does it not resemble a spectacular and unusual dance, full of grace and elegance?

Polihroniade-Kozlovskaya
Rio de Janeiro 1979

The position appears so drawn, that both players were hypnotized by this. They agreed a draw, assuming that the h-pawn would divert the black knight, and that without its help Black would be unable to queen the d-pawn. And yet Black could have won!

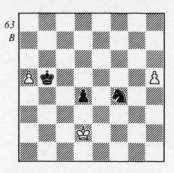

63
B

1	...	♔xa5

Not 1 ... ♘xh5? due to 2 a6! ♔xa6 3 ♔d3 with a draw.

2	h6	♔b5
3	h7	♘g6
4	♔d3	♔c5
5	♔e4!	♘h8!

Only a draw results from 5 ... ♔c4 6 ♔f5 ♘h8 7 ♔f6 d3 8 ♔g7. It was evidently this variation that the players had in mind when they concluded peace.

6	♔f5	

After 6 ♔d3 play could have continued: 6 ... ♔d5 7 ♔d2 ♔e4 8 ♔e2 d3+ 9 ♔d2 ♔d4 10 ♔d1 ♔e3 11 ♔e1 d2+ 12 ♔d1 ♘g6, when White is in zugzwang.

6	...	d3
7	♔f6	d2
8	♔g7	d1♕
9	♔xh8	♔d6!
10	♔g7	♔e7
11	h8♕	♕g4+

We have reached a text-book position, in which Black is able to win: 12 ♔h6 ♕h4+ 13 ♔g7 ♕g5+ 14 ♔h7 ♔f7.

Malchikov-Podgayets
USSR 1979

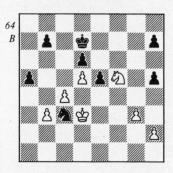

64
B

Black's extra pawn is not yet making itself felt. His king is passive, and the white b3-c4-d5 pawn wedge makes it hard for him to realize his advantage.

1	...	♘d1!
2	♔e2	♘b2
3	♔d2	a4!

The pawn chain is undermined at its base – correct strategy.

| 4 | ♔c2 | a3 |
| 5 | ♔b1 | b5! |

Forcing White to break up his pawn chain.

6	cb	♘d1
7	b6	♘c3+
8	♔a1	e4
9	♘e3	♔d8!!

The winning move – the position of the black king is of decisive

significance: 9 ... ♔c8? 10 ♘c4 ♔b7 11 ♘xd6+ ♔xb6 12 ♘c4+ ♔c5 13 ♘xa3, equalizing.

10	♘c4	♘xd5
11	♘xd6	e3
12	b7	♔c7
13	♘b5+	♔xb7
14	♘d4	

14 ♘xa3 ♘b4 is equally hopeless.

| 14 | ... | ♘c3 |
| 15 | ♘c2 | e2 |

0-1

BISHOP AGAINST KNIGHT

Play on both wings is an important strategic procedure in the struggle between a bishop and an enemy knight.

Arbakov-Gulko
Moscow 1981

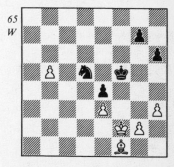

65
W

The passed b-pawn is a fairly weighty plus in White's position, but he cannot leave his kingside pawns to their fate by 'running' with his king to the queenside. In this situation he must combine play on both wings – only in this case will the advantage of bishop over knight become obvious.

1	♗c4	♘b6
2	♗f7!	

The routine 2 ♗b3 is weaker in view of 2 ... ♔e5 3 ♔g3 ♔f5 4 ♔h4 g6 5 g4+ ♔e5! 6 g5 h5 7 ♗d1 ♘c4 8 ♗xh5 gh 9 g6 ♘xe3 10 b6 ♔d6 11 ♔xh5 ♘f5! 12 ♔g4 e3, equalising. White transfers his bishop to c6, from where it attacks the e4 pawn, thus restricting the opponent's king.

2	...	♔f6
3	♗e8	♘c4
4	♗c6	♔f5
5	♔e2	♔e5
6	g4!	g6!

Black must not immobilize his kingside pawns. After 6 ... g5? the white king can calmly set off towards its passed pawn, using zugzwang to this aim: 7 ♗a8 ♘b6 8 ♗b7 ♘c4 9 ♗c6, when Black is forced to retreat his knight to b6, and he loses control over d2.

7	♔f2	

White waits, aiming to give his opponent the move.

7	...	♘b6
8	♔e1	h5

Or 8 ... ♘c4 9 ♔e2! h5 10 gh gh 11 h4 ♔f5 12 ♗d7+, and White wins.

9	gh	gh
10	h4	♔f5
11	♔d2	♔g4
12	♔c3	♔xh4
13	♔d4	♔g4

Not allowing White the chance of comfortably advancing his passed e-pawn: 13 ... ♔g3? 14 ♔xe4 h4 15 ♔f5.

14	♗xe4	h4
15	♔c5	♘a4+
16	♔c6	♔g3
17	♗d5	

The way for the e-pawn has to be cleared; Black was threatening to attack it from behind by 17 ... ♔f2.

17	...	♔f2

Black loses after 17 ... h3 18 b6 ♘xb6 19 ♔xb6 h2 20 ♔c5 ♔f2 21 ♔d4.

18	e4	♘c3
19	b6	h3
20	b7	h2
21	b8♕	h1♕
22	♕f4+!	

The most precise; after the less strong 22 ♕b2+ ♘e2 23 e5 ♕h8! Black can defend.

22	...	♔e2

22 ... ♔e1 is also hopeless in view of 23 ♕e3+ ♘e2 24 ♗c4.

23	♗c4+	♔d1
24	♕d6+	

1-0

24 ... ♔c1 is met by 25 ♕a3+, and 24 ... ♔e1 by 25 ♕g3+.

3 Unusual Balance of Forces

In the introduction we mentioned that there are three types of advantage – material, positional and psychological. But a number of positions also occur where there is a clash between different pieces. These are situations where, for example, one of the players is the exchange up, in return for which the other has one or two pawns, or where a rook is opposed by minor pieces, or a queen by rooks and minor pieces, and so on. This question is a fairly complicated one, and it is not our task to cover it in detail.

The positions which will be analyzed in this section are notable for the originality of their solutions, the paradoxical nature of their moves, in short, everything for which we love chess.

QUEEN AGAINST WEAKER PIECES

These fragments from two games by Lady World Champion Maya Chiburdanidze are a striking illustration of the playing methods in irrational positions, where the queen is both the heroine, and, alas, the victim.

Chiburdanidze-Akhmilovskaya
Candidates' Match, Tallinn 1977

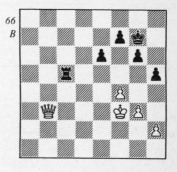

66
B

It is not by accident that this position finds its way into into a book about small advantages. Black has set up a fortress, which cannot be taken by storm, if in general at all. Very often the only winning method in such positions is the sacrifice of queen for rook, transposing into a favourable pawn ending. The most surprising thing is that a very similar position could have occurred in one of Botvinnik's games, and was analysed in detail by him. For the sake of clarity, let us reverse the colours of the pieces in the 'predecessor' and examine it.

Variation from the game
Troianescu-Botvinnik
Budapest 1952

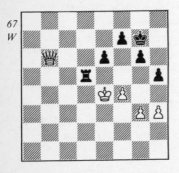

67
W

The positions are amazingly similar, aren't they? Virtual twins. The analysis of this ending has long been a classic, and there can be no doubt that both lady Candidates were familiar with the winning method demonstrated by Botvinnik.

1	g4	hg
2	hg	♔g8
3	♕c7	♔g7
4	♕c6	♔f8

White's king cannot be allowed onto the 5th rank, since its raid into the enemy rear would prove decisive: 4 ... ♖d1 5 ♕c3+ ♔g8 6 ♔e5 ♔g7 7 f5! ef 8 gf ♖f1 9 fg fg 10 ♔e6 etc.

| 5 | ♕a8+ | ♔g7 |

| 6 | ♕xd5 | ed+ |
| 7 | ♔xd5 | |

and the pawn ending is hopeless for Black. Let us check this, by playing through one of the main variations: 7 ... ♔f8 8 ♔d6 ♔e8 9 f5 g5 10 ♔c7 ♔e7 11 ♔c8! ♔d6 12 ♔d8, and White wins.

For this reason Akhmilovskaya chooses a different plan of defence for Black (instead of 1 ... ♖d5).

1	...	g5
2	fg	♖xg5
3	h3	♔h7
4	♔e4	♖d5
5	♕b8	♔g7
6	♕b2+	♔h7
7	♕b1!	

7 ♕f6 ♖f5+ 8 ♕xf5+ ef+ 9 ♔xf5 leads to a pawn ending which at first sight may appear won for White, but in fact Black can save it by 9 ... h4! 10 g4 ♔g7 11 ♔g5 f6+ 12 ♔xh4 ♔g6 13 ♔g3 f5, when a draw is inevitable.

Instead of 7 ♕b1, as played in the game, 7 g4 was also possible, aiming by the advance of the g-pawn to restrict the opponent and then invade with the king. Invade where? A very reasonable question, especially since there is only one answer to it – via the queenside! Let us see: 7 g4 hg 8 hg ♖g5 9 ♔f4 ♖g6 10 ♕e5! ♔g8 11 g5, and now it is evident that the black rook is tied to the g5 pawn, which means that it cannot prevent the white king from breaking through into the enemy rear. Note that 9 ... ♔g6 (instead of 9 ... ♖g6) is no better: 10 ♕h8 e5+ 11 ♔f3 e4+ 12 ♔f4! ♖c5 13 ♕g8+ ♔f6 14 g5+ ♔e7 15 g6, and Black's defences are breached.

	7	...	♔g7
	8	♕a1+	♔g6

8 ... ♔h7 is well met by 9 g4, aiming to carry out the plan given in the previous note.

9	♕h8	♖g5
10	♕g8+	♔f6
11	♕d8+	♔g6
12	♕f8!	

Exploiting the fact that the g3 pawn is indirectly defended – 12 ... ♖xg3? 13 ♕g8+ – White prevents the opponent from playing 12 ... ♔f6, which would lead to the loss of the h5 pawn: 13 ♕h6+ ♖g6 14 ♕xh5.

12	...	♖f5
13	g4	hg
14	hg	♖d5
15	♕g8+	♔f6
16	♕h8+	♔g6
17	♔f4	♖c5
18	♕g8+	♔f6
19	g5+	♔e7
20	g6	♖f5+
21	♔e4	fg
22	♕xg6	

and **Black resigned**, since a well known theoretical position, won for White, has been reached. First the black king is driven off the back rank, and then White's king breaks through from the rear to the e-pawn. Now the reader may be able to imagine how much tenacity and resourcefulness are required to win such an ending. Patience and hard work are the corner-stones of the difficult process of chess improvement.

Chiburdanidze-Dudkova
USSR 1976

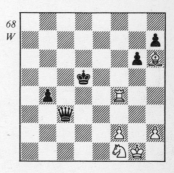

White has a slight material advantage, but the realizing of it is made difficult by the small number of forces remaining on the board. It is instructive to follow the virtuoso way in which Chiburdanidze co-ordinates her pieces and gains the win.

	1	♘e3+	♔e6

Not 1 ... ♔d6 due to 2 ♖xb4 and 3 ♗f8+.

	2	♖e4+!	♔d7

After 2 ... ♔f7 White wins by 3 ♖e7+ and 4 ♘d5.

	3	♖e7+!	♔c6

This simplifies things for White, but even after 3 ... ♚c8 there is a win as follows: 4 ♗f4 b3 5 ♘d5 ♕a1+ 6 ♚g2 b2 7 ♖c7+ ♚d8 8 ♗g5+ ♚e8 9 ♖e7+ ♚d8 10 ♖g7+ ♚e8 11 ♘c7+ ♚f8 12 ♘e6+, and mate next move.

4	♖c7+	♚xc7
5	♘d5+	♚d6
6	♘xc3+	bc
7	♚g2	♚d5
8	♚f3	♚c4
9	h4	♚b3
10	♚g4	c2
11	♗e3	

1-0

The following example shows a clash between a queen and two rooks. Activity and precise calculation are the requirements for success in this clash.

Stanciu-Vaisman
Romania 1978

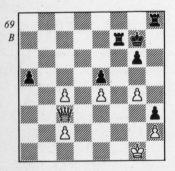

69
B

Two rooks are a more than sufficient material equivalent to a queen. And if they can be co-ordinated, things become very difficult for the queen. Here two of Black's pawns – at a5 and e5 – are attacked. They cannot both be defended simultaneously, that is obvious. Therefore it is very important now for Black to find a way of evacuating his rooks.

1	...	♖d8!
2	♕xh3	

Black was threatening mate, and so this pawn had to be eliminated.

2	...	♖d1+
3	♚g2	♖d2+
4	♚g1	

The king cannot advance – after 4 ♚g3 ♖df2 things are very tight for the white pieces.

4	...	♖b7
5	♕f1	♖b2
6	h4	♖bxc2
7	h5	

Now that the black rooks fully control the 2nd rank, White has only one chance of saving the game – to expose the position of the black king by the advance of his kingside pawns, and to try to give perpetual check. Black must be on the alert!

7	...	gh
8	gh	♚h6!!

The king fearlessly advances, under fire from the white queen. Black's optimism is based on precise calculation.

9 c5

Let us try checking the black king: 9 ♕f6+ ♔xh5 10 ♕xe5+ ♔g4 11 ♕f5+ ♔g3, and it becomes clear that there will be no perpetual check, whereas the king's activity has increased sharply.

9 ... ♖b2!

Taking the h-pawn would mean helping White – 9 ... ♔xh5? 10 ♕h3+.

10 ♔h1 ♖f2

11 ♕d3

Even worse is 11 ♕g1 ♔xh5 12 ♕d1+ ♔h4.

11 ... ♖bd2

12 ♕e3+ ♔h7

13 ♔g1 ♖fe2

0-1

ROOK OR MINOR PIECES?

Two minor pieces are stronger than a rook. This is arithmetically, translated into pawns. Everything depends, of course, on the special features of the position, on the concrete situation on the board.

Belyavsky-Dolmatov
USSR 1979

It is hard to believe that in this position Black has sufficient grounds for playing for a win. But the whole point is that White's pieces are disunited and poorly co-ordinated – the knight at h3 is unable to come to the aid of the bishop in its battle against the rook on the queenside. An exceptionally interesting and complicated battle develops, in which Dolmatov plays with great ingenuity and strength.

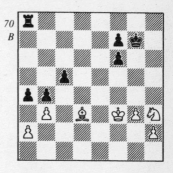

1 ... c4!!

Brilliantly played! Much weaker is 1 ... ♖h8? 2 ♘f2! ab 3 ab ♖xh2 4 ♘e4, when it is Black who must think in terms of equalizing.

2 ♗xc4

If 2 bc, then 2 ... ♖b8! with dangerous threats.

2 ... ♖c8!

Threatening 3 ... ♖xc4.

3 ♗d3 a3

4 ♔e3!

The king hurries to the aid of the bishop. 4 ♘f2 is less good, two typical variations being 4 ... ♖c1 5 h4 ♖a1 6 ♗c4 ♖xa2 7 ♘d3 ♖f2+ 8 ♔xf2 a2 9 ♘xb4 a1♕ 10 ♘d3 ♕h1!, or 4 ... ♖c3 5 h4 ♖xb3 6 ab a2 7 ♔g2 a1♕, with a decisive advantage to Black in both cases.

4 ... ♖c1!

This is stronger than 4 ... ♖c3 5 ♘f2!

5	♘f4	♖a1
6	♘d5	♖xa2
7	♘xb4	♖xh2
8	♗e2	♖h3!
9	♔f2	

It is weaker to defend the g-pawn from the third rank, since then Black wins the b3 pawn with check: 9 ♔f3 ♖h1 10 ♗d3 ♖a1! 11 ♘c2 ♖b1.

| 9 | ... | f5! |

Depriving the white bishop of the important e4 square.

10	♘a2!	f4
11	gf	♖xb3
12	♗c4	♖h3
13	♗f1	♖h2+
14	♗g2	♔f6
15	♔g3	♖h5!

The rook aims by the shortest path for the key squares b2 and c2.

16	♗f1	♖c5!
17	♗d3	♖d5
18	♗a6	♖d2
19	♗c4	♖d4

0-1

Gheorghiu-Honfi
Monte Carlo 1969 (71)

Formally material is equal, but the advantages of White's position are also obvious – Black's four pawns are blockaded, and his king and rook have little mobility. White's plan may involve the creation of a passed pawn on the queenside, and by skilfully manoeuvring he achieves his aim.

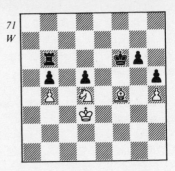

71
W

1	♗c7	♖b7
2	♗d8+	♔e5
3	♗g5	♖b6
4	♘f3+	♔e6

White wins more easily after 4 ... ♔f5 5 ♔d4 ♔e6 6 ♔c5!

| 5 | ♔d2! | |

In the following chapter we will talk in more detail about so-called psychological advantages, and here we will simply mention that in such endings, where one of the sides is forced to defend passively, the other may take his time, granting his opponent the 'right' to make a mistake.

| 5 | ... | ♖a6? |

Black should have patiently waited to see what White would do next – 5 ... ♖b7.

6	♘d4+	♔e5
7	♘xb5	♖b6
8	♘d4!	

A splendid reply – both pawn adn knight are immune.

8	...	♚e4
9	b5	♜b7
10	♚c3	♜b8
11	♗e7	♜e8
12	♘c6	♚f5
13	♚d4	♚e6
14	b6!	♜c8
15	b7	♜xc6
16	♗c5!	
	1-0	

ADVANTAGE OF THE EXCHANGE

We will conclude this section with some examples where one side is the exchange up. It stands to reason that the other side has compensation in the form of a pawn, or perhaps even two.

Moldoyarov-Sanchemov
Alma-Ata 1974

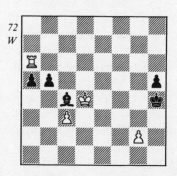

A prosaic position, wouldn't you agree? Black diverts the rook with his a-pawn, then picks up the

g-pawn with his king, and the draw is obvious. But this diagnosis proves faulty. White wins by force, by erecting an original mating construction.

    1   ♜g6!

Give up the g-pawn? Not for the world! This modest little pawn has a brilliant future!

1	...	a4
2	♚e3	a3
3	♚f4	a2
4	♜g3	♗e6

Now Black is all ready to obtain a new queen and win. For what has White been aiming?

5	♜h3+!!	♗xh3
6	g3 mate	

A fantastic finish!

S.Garcia-Padevsky
Varna 1971

It is difficult to imagine that White cannot save this game. After all, he has in reserve the sacrifice of his rook for the a-pawn, after which the white-squared h1 corner should rescue him. But by energetic play Black manages to realize his advantage.

1	...	♔g5
2	♔e4	h3
3	♖b3	

Kings, unfortunately, do not fly, otherwise the white king would long since have winged its way into the saving corner. The other rook move would also not have helped: 3 ♖a1 g3! 4 hg ♔g4.

| 3 | ... | ♗g1 |
| 4 | ♖a3 | |

The h-pawn cannot be defended: 4 ♖b2 g3!

| 4 | ... | ♗xh2 |
| 5 | ♖xa7 | ♗e5!! |

The path to victory is thorny – the carefree 5 ... ♗g3? would have allowed White to escape defeat miraculously: 6 ♖g7+! ♔h6 7 ♖g8! h2 8 ♖h8+ ♔g7 9 ♖h5 ♔g6 10 ♖h8 ♗e5! 11 ♖h4! g3 12 ♔f3.

| 6 | ♖d7 | |

6 ♖h7 is met by 6 ... g3!, while after 6 ♔xe5 h2 7 ♖g7+ ♔h6 8 ♖g8 ♔h7 the pawn cannot be stopped.

| 6 | ... | h2 |
| 7 | ♖d1 | ♗d4!! |

0-1

The finale to this little chess suite – the bishop sacrifices itself for the sake of the pawns!

Camilleri-Andersson
Raach 1970

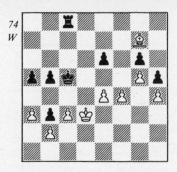

74
W

White has set up something of a fortress, which is by no means simple to break up. One thing is clear – Black must activate his rook and break through from the rear to the opponent's pawns. It is instructive to follow how subtly and originally Andersson solves this difficult problem.

1	♗d4+	♔d6
2	♗e5+	♔e7
3	♗f6+	♔f7

Where the king is heading for is a big secret!

| 4 | ♗d4 | ♖d8! |
| 5 | ♔e2 | |

The only move – Black meets 5 ♔e3 with 5 ... e5, and seizes either the d- or the f-file with his rook.

| 5 | ... | b4! |
| 6 | a4 | ♖d7! |

White is now forced to open the d-file – he has run out of useful moves.

7 &e5   bc
8 &xc3   ♖c7!

Clear the way for the b-pawn!

9 ♔d3   ♖c8

Once again White is faced with a difficult choice. The unusual 'dance' of the black rook is impressive.

10 ♔d4   e5+!
11 fe   ♔e6

The rook is ready to come into play along the f-file.

12 ♔d3

The unfortunate white king is fastened by a heavy chain to its bishop.

12 ...   ♖f8
13 &xa5   ♖a8!

Change of course!

14 &b4   ♖xa4
15 &a3   ♔xe5
16 ♔c3   ♖xe4
17 ♔xb3   ♖xh4
           0–1

The black rook has done an excellent job – the h-pawn is unstoppable.

Gufeld-Bagirov
USSR Championship 1963 *(75)*

With Black to move the win is not difficult: 1 ... ♖e1! 2 &c3 ♖e6 3 ♔f4 (3 &d2 c4 4 &e3 c3 5 ♔e2 ♖d6) 3 ... c4 4 ♔f5 ♔e7 5 f4 ♖e3, and the pawn queens. But in the diagram position it is White's move, and this enables him to approach the black pawn with his king.

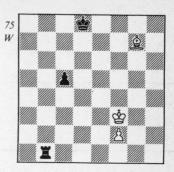

75
W

1 ♔e4   ♖d1
2 &f8!   c4
3 &b4   ♔d7
4 f4   ♖c1

The defence would have been more difficult after 4 ... ♖d3!, not allowing the bishop to go to c3.

5 ♔d4   ♔c6
6 &c3   ♔b5
7 f5   ♖d1+
8 ♔e4   ♔c5
9 f6   ♔d6
10 &e5+   ♔e6
11 &c3   ♖d3
12 &a1

The bishop has two free squares available along the long diagonal – a1 and b2. It cannot go to d4 or e5 because of ... ♖h3.

12 ...   ♔f7
13 &b2   ♔g8
14 &a1   ♔f8
15 &b2

And after a further 46 moves the games ended in a draw.

Pranitcki-Kaposztas
Romania 1977

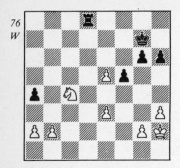

76
W

Can Black realize his advantage? Yes, but in order to win he has to work quite hard and find some far from obvious moves.

1	♔g3	♖c8
2	♘b6	a3!

By this piquant little combination Black achieves the elimination of all the queenside pawns.

3	ba	♖c3
4	♔f4	♖xa3
5	♘d5	♖a4+!

Otherwise White plays e6 and ♔e5.

6	♔f3	♖xa2
7	g4	♖a5
8	e4	♖a3+!
9	♘e3	

Forced: White cannot give up his h-pawn.

9	...	fg+!
10	hg	♔f7
11	g5!	

An interesting idea. White intends to set up a fortress, the approaches to which will be controlled by the knight.

11	...	hg!
12	♔f2	♔e6
13	♘g4	♖c3!
14	♔g2	

White must maintain his control of g3.

14	...	♖c7
15	♔f3	♖f7+
16	♔e3	♖f1!
17	♔d4	

17 ♔e2 would have lost to 17 ... ♖f4 18 ♘f2 ♔xe5 19 ♘d3+ ♔xe4.

17	...	♖g1
18	♘f2	g4
19	♘d3	♖d1!
20	♔e3	♖xd3+!

The transition into a pawn ending is the quickest way to win.

21	♔xd3	♔xe5
22	♔e3	g5!

0-1

Chigorin-Steinitz
World Championship Match
3rd Game, Havana 1889

77
W

It is not apparent how White

can realize his minimal advantage. Activity is required, but the black pieces have set up a very secure blockade. In addition, for the moment there is no real target for attack. And yet White finds one – the f5 pawn. Observe the virtuoso way in which Chigorin exploits the latent tactical possibilities in the position.

1	h5	gh
2	♗c2	♔e7
3	♖e5+	♔f8
4	♖xf5+	♔e7
5	♖e5+	♔d7
6	f3!	

It would of course be unfavourable for White to exchange his f-pawn for the h-pawn.

6	...	h4!
7	♔g4	♖g8+
8	♔xh4	♖g2

Black has managed to activate his forces somewhat, and in addition the white king is now not very well placed.

9	♗f5+	♔c6
10	b3!	♗f2+
11	♔h3	♖g3+
12	♔h2	♖xf3
13	♔g2	♖f4!

The ending after 13 ... ♖xf5 14 ♖xf5 ♘xf5 15 ♔xf2 is a technical win for White.

14 ♗e6!

14 ♖f1 allows Black to save the game: 14 ... ♘xf5! 15 ♖xf2 ♖xf2+ 16 ♔xf2 ♘d4 17 ♖e3 b5! 18 ♖d3

ba! 19 ba ♔c5.

14	...	♗c5
15	♗d5+	♔d7
16	♖e6	♘f5
17	♗c4+	♔c7
18	♖d3!	h5
19	♗b5	♖g4+
20	♔h2	♖h4+
21	♖h3	♗d6+
22	♔g2	♖g4+
23	♔f1!	♘g3+
24	♔f2	h4

It appears that Black can be quite satisfied with his position, but Chigorin skilfully suppresses the opponent's activity and seizes the initiative.

25	♖h6!	♖f4+
26	♔g2	♗e7
27	♖c6+	♔b7
28	♖c4	♖f8
29	♖d4	♔c8
30	♖d7	♗d8
31	♖h2!	♘e4
32	♖g7	♘c5
33	♖h3	♗f6
34	♖g6	♗d8
35	♗c4	♖f4
36	♖f3	♖d4
37	♖g7	♔b8

37 ... ♘xa4 is met by 38 ♗a6+.

38 ♖ff7

White has at last managed to co-ordinate his pieces.

38	...	♖d6
39	♔h3	♖d2
40	♖h7	♖d6
41	♗f1!	♘e6!

42	🜚d7!	🜚c6
43	♔g4	🜚c7
44	♗c4!	🜚xc4
45	bc	♔c8
46	🜚d6	♞c5
47	🜚c6+	♔b8
48	🜚h8	

1-0

48 ... ♞b7 49 ♔h3 is zugzwang.

Reshevsky-Fischer
New York 1961

78
B

Black must activate his pieces fully and aim to exploit his pawn majority on the kingside.

1	...	🜚d8!
2	🜚c2	

Black must not be allowed to co-ordinate his rook and knight.

2	...	🜚d3
3	🜚xb6	

3 🜚e2 🜚b3 is OK for Black.

3	...	🜚xe3
4	a5	f4

In advancing his pawns, Black at the same time creates threats against the opponent's king, thus gaining vital tempi.

| 5 | 🜚f2? | |

5 a6 would have led to a position of dynamic equilibrium, in which the most likely outcome is a draw, e.g. 5 ... f3+ 6 ♔f1 🜚d3 7 ♔e1 🜚e3+ 8 ♔f1 🜚d3.

5	...	♞xf2
6	♔xf2	🜚e4!
7	b4	🜚e3!

Black has as though 'urged on' the opponent's pawns, with the aim of attacking them with his rook from the rear.

8	a6	🜚a3
9	🜚c6	g5
10	hg+	hg
11	b5	

White's passed pawns are further advanced, but Black has it all precisely worked out.

11	...	g4
12	🜚c8	♔f5
13	b6	g3+
14	♔e1	

At g2 the king ends up in a mating net: 14 ♔g2 🜚a2+ 15 ♔h3? 🜚h2 mate, or 15 ♔f1 f3.

14	...	🜚a1+
15	♔e2	g2
16	🜚f8+	♔e4
17	🜚xf4+	

Clever, but insufficient.

17	...	♔xf4
18	b7	g1♛

More efficient was the thematic 18 ... ♔e4! 19 b8♛ 🜚a2+, with inevitable mate.

After a few more moves, realising that there was no perpetual check, **White resigned**.

4 Psychological Advantage

It is quite possible that this heading may provoke a sceptical smile on the part of some of the readers. The fact that an advantage may be material, positional, or a combination of these two forms, we know perfectly well, but a psychological advantage . . . Rather than draw any hasty conclusions, we will do better to hand over to a specialist in the field of chess psychology. This is what grandmaster Nikolai Krogius, Doctor of Psychological Sciences, writes:

"In chess, as in other spheres of human activity, there are two aspects – objective and subjective. These aspects cannot be set off one against the other, nor in chess can one take account only of its objective aspect, only its scientific theory – the laws and principles of this theory are employed in practice by living people, who may be similar or different . . ."

Let us turn to some examples.

**Eingorn-Chiburdanidze
Odessa 1982**

79
B

The position is objectively drawn, but playing it for White is a fairly disagreeable business – to draw he has to make the best moves, whereas at the same time his opponent is practically risking nothing. In such situations the probability of a mistake by the weaker side increases considerably. These mistakes may be associated with certain traits of character. If a player is tenacious, and is sufficiently strong-willed and composed, he can hope for a successful defence. If one of these necessary components is missing, the end result may prove dismal.

There is one more interesting and highly characteristic detail. If he fails to win a won position, any player is of course upset – it is a vexing loss of half a point. But even greater distress is caused by losing an objectively drawn position. The loss in points in the two cases is identical, but it is undoubtedly more difficult to accept the defeat.

From the mathematical viewpoint all this seems paradoxical an and illogical, but chess is played by people and not machines (machines fulfil the will of the people). Emotions sometimes have a stronger effect on a person's psyche than obvious facts. In the example under consideration, Eingorn, a young and highly promising master, was unable to cope with the psychological burden, and as a result suffered a vexing defeat.

1	...	♔d4!
2	♔f3	♔d5·
3	♘c6+	♔d3

For the moment White does everything correctly; weaker is 4 f5 g5! 5 h4 h6 with advantage to Black.

4	...	b4
5	♘a5	♘e7!

The knight aims for c6.

6	♘b3?	

6 ♘b7! would have led to a draw. The position of the knight at b3 allows Black to gain an important tempo.

6	...	♔c3

7	♘c5	♔c4
8	♘e4	♔d4
9	♘d2	♘g8!
10	♘b3+	♔d5
11	f5	gf
12	g5	♘e7
13	♔f4	

If 13 h5, the spectacular 13 ... ♘g6! is decisive.

13	...	♘g6+
14	♔xf5	♘xh4+
15	♔g4	♘g6
16	♔h5	♘f8
17	♔h6	♔c4
18	♘d2+	♔c3
19	♘e4+	♔d4
20	♘d2	♘e6
21	♘b3+	♔c4
22	♘c1	♔d4
23	♘b3+	♔d3
24	♔xh7	♘xg5+
25	♔g6	♘e6
26	♔f6	♔c3
27	♘a5	♘d8!
28	♔f5	♘c6!
29	♘b7	♔d4!
30	♘d6	b3
31	♘b5+	♔d3
32	♘a3	b2
33	♔e6	♘d4+!

0-1

Bangiev-Bilunov
Moscow 1971 *(80)*

White has a slight positional advantage, resulting from his two bishops and his somewhat superior pawn formation on the queenside.

It is advantageous for him to aim for the exchange of the rooks, after which his king may be able to break through to the queenside. Some subtle positional manoeuvring now commences.

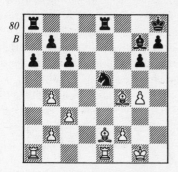

80
B

1	...	♖e6
2	♗e3	♖ae8
3	♖ed1	h6
4	♖d2	♔h7
5	♖ad1	g5
6	♖d8!	

The exchange of rooks favours White.

6	...	♗f6
7	♖xe8	♖xe8
8	♗b6	♗g7
9	♔f1	♗f6
10	♖d6	♔g7
11	♗d4	

White has acquired another small plus – an active rook.

11	...	♖e7
12	♗e3	♖d7?

A typical mistake in such endings!

By his unhurried play (♗b6-d4-e3) White has 'lulled' his opponent. A basic rule of the endgame is – do not not hurry! A very apt description of this was given by Sergey Byelavyenets:

". . . To many, the rule of 'do not hurry' may seem paradoxical, but in fact it is seen in practically all the endings of games by great masters of the endgame. Look carefully at the endings of Capablanca and Flohr, and you will see with what slowness, sometimes bordering on tedium, they realize an advantage . . . The repetition of moves in the endgame plays an important role. Disregarding the fact that it gains time for thinking, it can be mentioned that, by repeating moves, the active side acquires certain psychological gains. The defender, whose position is inferior, often cannot stand it, and creates a further weakening which eases his opponent's task . . . ."

13	♖xd7+	♘xd7
14	♗d3	♔f7
15	♔e2	♔e8
16	♗f5	♔d8
17	♔d1	♔c7
18	♔c2	♗e5?

It was better to wait with 18 ... ♗g7, keeping e5 free for the knight.

19	♔d3	♘f6

Alas, the e5 square is occupied . . .

20	♗d4	

An advantage of the two bishops is that often one of them can be exchanged with the aim of further activating the remaining forces.

20	...	♗xd4
21	♔xd4	♔d6
22	c4	b6
23	c5+	♔c7
24	♗e6	bc+
25	bc	♔d8
26	♔e5	♔e7
27	b4	h5
28	gh	♘xh5
29	♗c4	g4
30	♗xa6	g3
31	fg	♘xg3

Black has given up a pawn, but during this time he has managed to exchange all the kingside pawns. Now White's winning plan may be associated with either trapping the black knight, or a pawn breakthrough.

32	♗d3	♘h5
33	♗e4	♔d7
34	♗f5+	♔c7

34 ... ♔e7 is not possible due to 35 b5 cb 36 c6 ♔d8 37 ♔d6, winning.

35	♗g4!	

Now White's chief motto is the attack on the knight.

35	...	♘g3

Otherwise the knight is lost.

36	♔f4	♘f1
37	♗e2	♘d2
38	♔e3	♘b1

39	♔d3	♘a3
40	♔c3	♔d7
41	♔b2	♘b5
42	♗xb5	

1-0

White's persistence and purposefulness in this game were fully rewarded.

The games of former World Champion Mikhail Botvinnik are sometimes called 'an encyclopaedia of the art of chess'. In his ability to exploit psychological factors in the chess struggle, he can be placed alongside Emanuel Lasker.

Suetin-Botvinnik
Moscow 1952

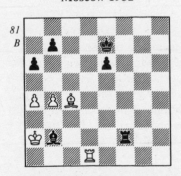

81
B

In this theoretically drawn position a certain accuracy and care are required of White. There is a psychological advantage on Black' side – he is in no danger of losing, and can hope to exploit inaccuracies in his opponent's play.

1	...	a5
2	ba	♗c3+
3	♔b3	♗xa5
4	♗b5	b6
5	♔c4	♔f6
6	♔d4	♖f4+
7	♔e3	♔e5
8	♖h1	♖e4+
9	♔d3	♖g4
10	♖h5+	♔d6
11	♖h8	♔e5
12	♖h5+	♔f4

Black waits, so as to gain time on the clock before the next control.

13	♖h3	♖g8
14	♖h4+	♔e5
15	♖h5+	♔d6
16	♖h4?!	

'Lulled' by the simplicity of the position, White commits his first inaccuracy. It was essential to defend the 3rd rank with his rook. But how could Suetin imagine that his king would end up in a mating net in the very middle of the board?

16	...	♖g3+
17	♔e4?!	

The king is doing nothing here, and should have gone to d4. But White's play is affected by the stereotype of an optical illusion – on a white square he thinks that his king will feel more comfortable.

17	...	♗d2
18	♗d3?	

Strangely enough, this natural move loses the game. It was not yet too late to play 18 ♔d4 or 18 ♖h5. The mistake was at hand, and White 'found' it.

18	...	♗g5!
19	♖h5	

Otherwise after 19 ... ♖g4+ the a-pawn is lost.

19	...	♔c5!

The white king is trapped. The mate can be avoided only by going into a hopeless pawn ending: 20 ♔e5 ♖xd3 21 ♖xg5 ♖d5+ etc.

0-1

Kotov-Botvinnik
Moscow 1955

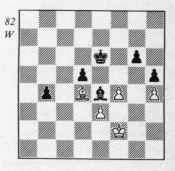

82
W

It is evident that Black's extra pawn is insufficient for a win. There is only one thing for him to 'latch' on to – the h4 pawn, but White can easily defend it with his bishop from f6, and it is not apparent what more can be done. But there is no point in agreeing a draw if there is even the slightest chance of victory, and Black

continues playing with maximum
energy.

1	♔e2	♚f5
2	♔d2	♚g4
3	♗f6	♚g3
4	♗e7	♚h3!

Of course, White cannot give up
his h-pawn, which means that the
black b-pawn is indirectly defended.

5	♗f6	♚g4
6	♗e7	♗f5!

The bishop must be transferred
to e6, so as then to advance the
pawn to b3. However, White is
still able to hold the draw.

7	♗f6	♚f3!
8	♗e7	b3
9	♔c3	♗e6!

The win of a second pawn
would have led to a clearly drawn
position after 9 ... ♚xe3 10 ♔xb3
♚xf4 11 ♔c3 ♚e3 12 ♗g5+ ♚e4
13 ♔d2.

11 ♗c5? (83)

Why did White make this losing
move? Remember that to 7 ...
♚f3! we attached an exclamation
mark without explanation. In
fact this was a subtle psychological
trap, into which White falls. He is
under the illusion that his bishop,
not having to worry about the h4
pawn, can permit itself a certain
freedom of movement. Possibly
10 ♔d2 seemed risky to White,
but it in fact would have saved the
game: 10 ... b2 11 ♔c2 ♚xe3 12

♔xb2 ♚xf4 13 ♔c3.

After this mistake by White,
Black brilliantly exploits the fact
that the opponent's bishop has left
the d8-h4 diagonal.

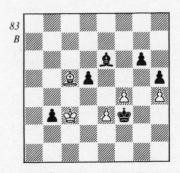

10	...	g5!!
11	fg	d4+!!
12	ed	

White also loses after 12 ♗xd4
♚g3 13 g6 ♚xh4 14 ♔d2 ♚h3! 15
♗f6 h4 16 ♚e2 ♚g2.

12	...	♚g3!

How strikingly the position has
changed? How are Black's passed
pawns to be stopped? Note that
Black must approach the h4 pawn
only via g3, not allowing White
the possibility of saving the game
by d5 and ♗f2, which could have
followed in reply to 12 ... ♚g4.

13	♗a3	♚xh4
14	♔d3	♚xg5
15	♚e4	h4
16	♚f3	♗d5+

0-1

5 The Game Ended in a Draw . . .

Admit now, do you often play through games, at the end of which is the laconic indication ½-½? Probably not. And games which are annotated also most often end in a decisive result. To a certain extent this is right. Chess, apart from anything else, and perhaps most importantly, is a struggle, and in it a winner is determined. But what if attack and defence are worthy of each other, if the subtle ideas of one player are parried by the no less subtle replies of the other? Then the winner is . . . chess! And the game ends in a draw.

How many dramatic clashes are at times concealed behind that laconic inscription ½-½! A player may have needed half a point more to go through to the next stage of an elimination cycle, or to achieve a grandmaster norm, or . . .

It stands to reason that in our discussions there is no place for so-called 'grandmaster' draws, which we all find pretty irritating. We will be talking about chess clashes where there is a full-blooded struggle, the intensity of which is often greater than in games with a decisive result.

First of all, here are a few examples of missed draws and missed wins. Any active chess player will, alas, be well familiar with the word 'missed' . . .

Nikolayevsky-Gufeld
Kiev 1951

84
W

White played the unreasonably sharp 1 b4, and after 1 ... cb 2 ab ♘xc4 he went on to lose. But meanwhile he could have saved the game, by exploiting the cramped position of the black king!

1   ♘c1!   g6!

2   ♘e2!!

The attempt to create counter-play by 2 ♔e5 meets with an exceptionally fine refutation: 2 ... ♔xg5 3 ♔d5 ♔f4 4 b4 ♔e3!! 5 ba g5 6 ♘a2 ♔d2!, and the white pieces are not able to stop the g-pawn.

2	...	♘xb3
3	♘g3+	♔h4
4	♘f5+!	♔h5
5	♘g3+	♔h4
6	♘f5+	♔h5

Draw! Black has to reconcile himself to this – if 6 ... gf, then 7 g6 ♘d4 8 ♔e5 ♘c6+ 9 ♔d6 ♘d8 10 ♔d7!, while 6 ... ♔h3 is met by 7 ♘e7!

An amazing possibility, which, alas, remained unrealized.

**Bronstein-Aronin
Leningrad 1947**

85
W

David Bronstein has always been distinguished by the originality of his ideas, and by his ability to find a concealed combinational blow, or to prepare a cunning

trap. In this game too he decided to catch his opponent in a trap, thus rejecting the more reliable plan of the lengthy and painstaking realization of his slight material advantage. What resulted from this, we will now see.

1	♔h3?!	♗xa3
2	♘e7+	♔xf4
3	♘g6+	

That seems to be it, the game is over . . . That is in fact what the master playing Black decided. After the feeble 3 ... ♔g5 he soon lost the game. And yet Black had a study-like way to save it!

3	...	♔e3!
4	♘xf8	♗xb4
5	♖e6+	

All these moves are forced. 5 ♖f6 is no better for White in view of 5 ... ♗xf8 6 ♖xf8 ♔xd3, when Black's passed pawns on the queenside guarantee him a draw.

5	...	♔xd3
6	♘d7	♗c3
7	♖xa6	b4
8	♖b6	♔c4!
9	♖c6+	♔d5!
10	♖c8	♗d4!
11	♔xh4	b3
12	♖b8	♔c4!

The only move. The impulsive 12 ... b2 loses to 13 ♘b6+ and 14 ♘a4.

| 13 | ♔g4 | b2 |
| 14 | ♔f3 | ♔d3! |

And a draw is inevitable. What

a pity that such an interesting idea was not put into practice.

Sakharov-Vasyukov
Alma-Ata 1969

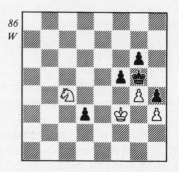

86
W

It appears that White has no reason to think in terms of winning – there is too little material on the board. And yet there is a win, but about that later. First let us see what happened in the game.

1	gf	♚xf5
2	♘e3+	♚e5
3	♔g4	♚d4
4	♘d1	♚e4
5	♘b2	d2
6	♘d1	♚e5!
7	♘f2	♚e6
8	♔xh4	♚f5
9	♔g3	g5
10	♔f3	♚g6!
11	♔e2	♚h5
12	♔xd2	♚h4
13	♔e1	♚g3
14	♔f1	♚h2!

½-½

2 ♘e3? was a mistake – unfortunately, it was the wrong piece that went to this square. White could have won, by exploiting the possibility of ... a mating idea! Here is a sample variation: 2 ♔e3! g5 3 ♔f3 ♚e6 4 ♔g4 ♚f6 5 ♘d2 ♚g6 6 ♘e4 ♚h6 7 ♔f5 ♚h5 8 ♘f6+ ♚h6 9 ♘g4+ ♚h5 10 ♔f6!! d2 11 ♔g7 d1♛ 12 ♘f6 mate!

The complete triumph of mind over matter!

There is also another winning possibility in the initial position: 1 ♘d2! fg+ 2 hg ♔f6 3 ♔f4! ♚e6 4 ♘e4 ♚d5 5 ♔e3 ♚e5 6 ♘d2 h3 7 ♘f3+ ♔f6 8 ♚xd3 h2 9 ♘xh2 ♚g5 10 ♔e3 ♚h4 11 ♔f3 – the white knight and king have worked well, and the win is now not far off.

Gufeld-Augustin
Sochi 1979

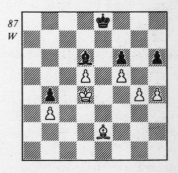

87
W

For the moment the white bishop has no scope, and this factor aids Black's defence. The activation of his bishop is White's immediate task. Only after this can he set in motion his passed pawns. One – the d-pawn, we can see, but where is the second? The f-pawn will become the second after the g4-g5 breakthrough.

1 &f1   &e7

For the moment Black's bishop cannot lift the blockade – 1 ... &g3 2 g5! fg 3 hg hg 4 &h3 &e7 5 &c5.

2 &h3!   &e8
3 &c4   &d8
4 &b5   &c7
5 g5!   fg
6 hg   hg
7 f6   &e5
8 f7   &d6

What is White to do now? To create a second passed pawn, he has sacrificed a pawn, and the position has simplified considerably. To White's aid · comes zugzwang – the 'magic wand' of many endings.

9 &e6!

The direct 9 &c4? does not succeed: 9 ... &d8 10 &d4 &e7 11 &e6 g4!

9 ...   &f8

Now 9 ... g4 does not work: 10 &xg4 &f8 11 &c4 &d6 12 &e6 &d8 13 &d3! &e7 14 &d4!, and Black is in zugzwang.

10 &c4   &d8
11 &d4   &e7
12 &e5   g4
13 d6+

The simple 13 &f4 is also sufficient to win.

13 ...   &d8
14 &xg4??

After achieving an absolutely won position, White blunders, overlooking the possibility of stalemate.

He could have won by 14 &d5 g3 15 &h3 &h6 16 &c4 &f8 17 &c5.

14 ...   &xd6+!

½-½

15 &xd6 leads to a highly amusing stalemate.

Kasparian-Akshanov
Tbilisi 1931

88
W

The pawns are all on one wing, which considerably hinders White in the realization of his advantage. In addition, his queen and rook are not altogether well placed, being tied down by the opponent's queen. Here White should have regrouped by ♕e7 and ♖d5-d7, when he retains winning chances.

But Kasparian decided to conclude the game with a direct attack. Outwardly everything seems to favour this – both the advanced position of Black's pawns, and the passivity of his rook. But chess is truly inexhaustible – a saving line is found.

| 1 | g4 | hg |
| 2 | h5 | ♕c3! |

An excellent resource! Now the white king too comes under attack.

3	hg	♕h3+
4	♔g1	g3!
5	gf+	♔h7

Have you already noticed the outlines of a stalemate? There is a draft, but the canvas is not yet complete . . .

| 6 | fg |

Two extra pawns in the rook ending do not guarantee success, since one of them is quickly lost.

6	...	♕xg3+
7	♔f1	♕d3+!
8	♔g2

A long journey awaits the king.

8	...	♕e2+
9	♔h3	♕e3+
10	♔g4	♕g1+
11	♔f5	♕f1+
12	♔e6	♕a6+
13	♔e7	♕b7+!

The wonderful picture could still have been spoiled by a crude stroke: 13 ... ♕a3+ 14 ♕d6 ♖xf7+ 15 ♔xf7 ♕xd6 16 ♖h5+.

14	♔xf8	♕c8+
15	♔e7	♕d7+!
	½-½

Isn't such a draw a splendid thing?

Activity and once again activity – this is the motto by which the defence is conducted in the following examples.

Sergievsky-Hasin
USSR 1978

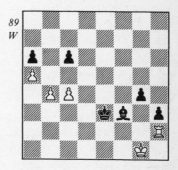

89
W

White's position looks very difficult – it only requires Black to play ... ♗e2, and the game will be beyond saving. White's only chance is an immediate breakthrough on the queenside and the activating of his rook.

1	b5!	cb
2	cb	ab
3	a6	b4
4	a7	♗e4
5	a8♕!

This looks like suicide – the a-pawn seemed to be White's only hope. But he has precisely worked everything out.

5	...	♗xa8
6	♖b2	g3
7	♖b3+	♔f4
8	♖xb4+	♗e4
9	♖b2	

½-½

Gufeld-Mikhalchishin
Tbilisi 1979

90
B

We have here a balance of forces which occurs very rarely in practice. Note the possibility of sacrificing the rook for the black-squared bishop, which is the theme of Black's defence.

1	...	♖a5+!

2 ♗xa5 ba leads to a theoretically drawn position.

2	♔d6	♖a3!
3	♗g6+	

The position is not essentially changed by 3 ♗c4+ ♔f8.

3	...	♔g8
4	♗d4	g4

This pawn eases Black's defence – White is forced to keep an eye on it.

5	♔e6	♖a4!

Not a minute's peace for the bishop! In the event of 5 ... ♖f3 Black loses spectacularly – 6 h6 ♖h3 7 ♗g7 g3 8 ♔f6 g2 9 h7+! ♖xh7 10 ♗f7 mate *(91)*.

This rare mating finish deserves a diagram.

91
B

Let us return to the game.

6	♗e5	♖a5!
7	♗d4	♖a4
8	♗f6	♖a2
9	h6	♖e2+
10	♔d6	♖h2
11	h7+	

½-½

Vladimirov-Novopashin

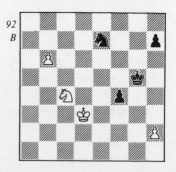

92
B

The two sides' passed pawns are obviously not of equal worth. Whereas the white pawn is extremely dangerous, Black's can be stopped by both king and knight. However, the utmost accuracy is required of White to realize his advantage.

1	...	♔f5
2	♞a5	♞d5
3	b7	♞b4+
4	♔e2!	

White must blockade the f-pawn, and then set about eliminating it.

4	...	♞a6
5	♔f3	♞b8
6	h4!	♔e5
7	♞b3	♞c6
8	♞c5	♔f5
9	♞d3!	

White can win the knight, but in doing so he loses any chance of winning the game – 9 ♞d7 ♞d4+ 10 ♔f2 ♞c6 11 b8♕ ♞xb8 12 ♞xb8 ♔g4.

9	...	♞d4+
10	♔f2	♞c6
11	♞b4!	♞b8
12	♔f3	♔e5

12 ... ♞d7 is met by 13 ♞d3.

13	♞d3+	♔d6
14	♔xf4	♔c6
15	♔g5	♔xb7
16	♔h6	♞c6
17	♔xh7	

And so, White has an extra rook's pawn (the only pawn left!)

in a knight ending. Can he manage to queen it? This task is a very difficult one.

17	...	♞e7
18	h5	♔c6
19	♔g7	♔d5
20	♔f6	♞g8+
21	♔f7	♞h6+
22	♔g7	♞f5+!

On 22 ... ♞g4 White wins by 23 ♞f2!

| 23 | ♔f6 | ♔e4! |

The culminating point. A decisive strengthening of White's position has to be found, and here too zugzwang comes to his aid. With this aim he should have played 24 ♔g6!, when it is not difficult to see that Black can no longer save the game, for example: 24 ... ♞h4+ 25 ♔g5 ♞f3+ 26 ♔f6!, or 24 ... ♞e7+ 25 ♔g5 ♞f5 26 ♞f2+ ♔e5 27 ♞g4+ ♔e4 28 ♞e3!

However, the move chosen by White also does not throw away the win, but it makes it rather more complicated.

24	♔g5	♞d6
25	♞f2+	♔e5
26	♔g6	♞f5
27	♞d3+	♔e4
28	♞c1?	♔f4
29	♞e2+	♔g4
30	♞g3	♞e7+
31	♔f6	♞f5!

½-½

But where is the promised win,

and at what point did White finally let it slip? Instead of 28 ♘c1 he should have played 28 ♔f6! ♘h6 29 ♔g7 ♘f5+ 30 ♔g6! (triangulation!), and he reaches the position after 24 ♔g6! in which, as we have seen, Black is helpless.

In the following game White is in an inferior position, but he finds clever counterplay based on the unfortunate position of the enemy king.

Ritov-Averkin
Tallinn 1967

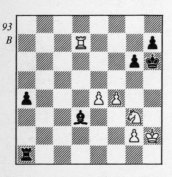

93
B

Black's outside passed a-pawn appears much more dangerous than its white opponent on the e-file. But here two important factors should be pointed out – Black's bishop is very insecure, and the position of his king at h6 gives White grounds for combinational play. And so an interesting struggle develops.

1	...	♗b5
2	♖b7	♗c4
3	♖c7	♗b3
4	♖b7	

This pursuit of the opponent's bishop is a necessary link in White's plan of defence.

4	...	♗g8
5	♖a7	a3
6	♘h1	

The knight aims for g4 and arrives there at just the right time!

| 6 | ... | a2 |
| 7 | ♘f2 | ♗e6 |

The threat of 8 ♘g4 is highly unpleasant, and Black has to forestall it.

8 g4!

Again threatening mate.

8	...	♗g8
9	g5+	♔h5
10	♖a3!	♗e6
11	♖a7	♗g8
12	♖a3	♗e6

½-½

Drawn by repetition of moves. But couldn't Black have played more strongly somewhere, e.g. 11 ... ♗f7? A simple analysis shows that this would have turned out dismally for him: 12 ♖xf7 ♖h1+ 13 ♔xh1 a1♕+ 14 ♔h2 ♕h8 15 ♖a7!, and White wins.

Miller-Weltmander
USSR 1949

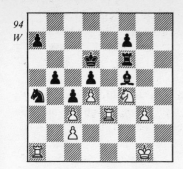

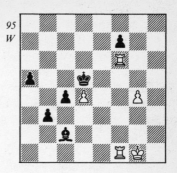

Here the defending side's counter-play is based on the strength of far-advanced passsed pawns. Positional manoeuvring does not promise White success, since his queenside pawns are chronically weak. Therefore he begins a combination with the aim of exploiting the somewhat unfortunate position of the black pieces on the f-file.

1	♘xd5	♔xd5
2	♖f1!	

Against the threat of g4 there appears to be no satisfactory defence, and it seems that White must win, but now comes a brilliant counter-combination by Black.

2	...	a5!
3	g4	♘xc3!!

Black's bishop is attacked, and yet he sacrifices another piece!

4	♖xc3	b4
5	♖cf3	♗xc2
6	♖xf6	b3 *(95)*

A unique position! White has an enormous material advantage, but he cannot win due to the strength of Black's passed pawns.

7	♖a6	♔xd4
8	♖xa5	b2
9	♖b5	c3
10	♖b8	♗d3
11	♖e1	♔c5
12	♔f2	♗b5
13	♖e5+	♔d6!
14	♖exb5	c2
15	♖xb2	c1♕

½-½

**Azmaiparashvili-Yeolyan
USSR 1979**

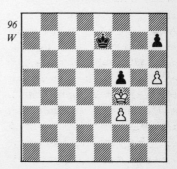

Is it really possible for something unusual to happen in this ultra-simple position? That's what you are thinking, isn't it? You will now witness mistakes by both these young masters, and will discover that, in spite of its simplicity, the position harbours a number of hidden pitfalls.

1 &g5?

One really shouldn't seek too much of a good thing – the obvious 1 &xf5 would have won: 1 ... &f7 2 f4! &e7 3 &e5 &f7 4 &d6! &f6 5 h6! &g6 6 &e6.

| 1 | ... | &f8 |
| 2 | &xf5 | &f7?? |

Black as though forgets that, apart from direct opposition there is also knight's opposition, and he rejects the gift of fate: 2 ... &e7! 3 &g5 &f7 4 &h6 &g8 5 f4 &h8, and the black king is ready to stalemate itself.

3 &g4?

And straight away – a mistake in return. By 3 f4! he could have transposed into the variation given in the note to White's 1st move.

3	...	&f6
4	&f4	&f7
5	&f5	&e7

After much 'groping in the dark', Black has nevertheless found the saving path.

| 6 | &e5 | &f7 |
| 7 | &d6 | |

Had White's pawn been at f4, this move would have led to a win.

7	...	&f6
8	&d7	&f7
9	h6	&g6!

Black would have lost after 9 ... &f6? 10 &e8 &g6 11 f4 &xh6 12 &f7.

| 10 | f4 | &f7! |
| 11 | f5 | &f6 |

½-½

A possible finish: 12 &e8 &xf5 13 &f7 &e5 14 &g7 &e6 15 &xh7 &f7. An ending of many mistakes!

Rittner-Tile
Correspondence 1971

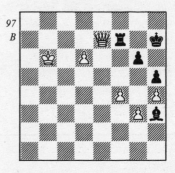

97
B

It is obvious that the d-pawn is White's main trump, since on the kingside Black has set up a fortress. The white queen is ready to sacrifice itself, but it cannot be accepted: 1 ... &xe7 2 de &d7 3 &c7 &a4 4 &d8 &g7 5 e8& &xe8 6 &xe8, and the pawn ending is hopeless for Black.

| 1 | ... | &g8! |

2	♔c7	♖g7!!
3	♔d8	

After 3 ♕xg7+ ♔xg7 4 d7 ♗xd7 5 ♔xd7 ♔f7 the white king cannot break through to the opponent's pawns.

3	...	♖f7!
4	♔e8	♖g7!

A paradoxical situation – White has approached right up to the black king, but there is no win. Hurrah for the geometry of the chessboard!

5	♕e5	♗d7+
6	♔d8	♗g4
7	♕e8+	♔h7
8	d7	♗f5!

For the moment the d-pawn is immune, for if 8 ... ♗xd7? 9 ♕xd7 ♖xd7+ 10 ♔xd7 ♔g7 11 ♔e7.

9	♔c7	♗xd7
10	♕xd7	♔g8!
11	♔d6	♖xd7+
	½-½!	

This game did not in fact end in a draw, but even so . . .

Tal-Gufeld
Yurmala 1977 *(98)*

In the heat of the battle Black one by one lost all his pawns, but he intends to continue the struggle to the last bullet (that is to say – bishop). He threatens 1 ... ♗e5. However, Black's initiative is not of course worth four pawns. After

1 ♘c4 (there is no need to be greedy!) 1 ... ♖xc2 2 d6 ♗d7 3 ♗d4 ♗c6+ 4 ♔g1 White would have been bound to win. But in the game the former World Champion unexpectedly made a mistake, and the struggle flared again with new strength.

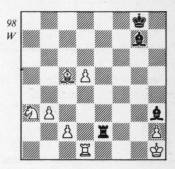

98
W

1	♖d3?	♖e1+
2	♗g1	♗f5!
3	♖e3	♖a1!
4	♘c4	♗d4
5	♖g3+	♔h7
6	h4	♖c1!
7	♘d2	

White's forces are tied up hand and foot. Black would have answered 7 ♔h2 with 7 ... ♗e4!

7	...	♗xc2

The ranks of white infantry begin to thin out . . .

8	d6	♖d1!
9	♘c4	♗f2!

But not 9 ... ♗xb3? 10 ♖xb3 ♗xg1 due to 11 ♖b7+ ♔h6 12 ♔g2, when White has good winning chances.

10	♖g4

No better is 10 ♖g2 ♗e4 11 ♔h2 ♗xg2 12 ♗xf2 ♗d5 (or 12 ... ♗c6) with a probable draw.

10	...	♗xb3
11	♘b2	♗d5+
12	♔h2	♗xg1+
13	♖xg1	♖d2+
14	♔g3	

The draw has become completely obvious, and Black only needed to play 14 ... ♗b3 or 14 ... ♗e6. But at this point his nerve gave out.

14	...	♖xb2??
15	d7	♖b8
16	♖d1	♖g8+
17	♔f4	♗e6
18	d8♕	♖xd8
19	♖xd8	

The game was adjourned, but Black resigned without resuming (in the final position White wins following analysis by Averbakh, published in his book on rook against minor piece endings).

Yes, in the merciless game of chess, you have to be vigilant to the very end!